ANTHOLOGY 2019

Stories Of The Struggle For Education And Equality In Malawi

VoiceFlame

Mary Tuchscherer

Published in the United States

by

VoiceFlame

Edited by Lizabeth Rogers

Graphic layout by Lizabeth Rogers

All photos courtesy of VoiceFlame

Graphics by Katyau courtesy of Adobe Stock

Available in paperback and ebook format through Amazon

ISBN: 9781799090137

Published January 1, 2019

www.VoiceFlame.org

ANTHOLOGY
2019

Pamela,
Thank you for
your continued
support of
women's voices!
Love!
Mary

Dedication

This book is dedicated to you, the women and girls of Malawi, Africa and elsewhere who struggle to receive the education that is rightfully yours.

May you know your awesome brilliance and celebrate the abundant contributions that you bestow on the world.

This collection of life stories gives voice to Malawian girls and women you may not have heard of, living, working and studying in Malawi against harrowing odds, from social, economic, and health challenges. It shows the candid stories of women using the written word to write a better future for themselves. They write not for your pity, but to show other girls in similar positions to keep focused on their goals despite the restrictions.

A truly inspiring read, written by the women in their own words. Stories about women who went from village girl to PHD lecturer, from orphan to manager at a young age, these stories happen under our noses, and it is time that a light is shone on them.

The highlight of every true life story is that to be able to bring you these stories, they had firstly unquenchable drive, a flame, and secondly they had someone encouraging and supporting them, be it a family member, mentor, or the organisers of this anthology. It is a lesson not just for women, but those who are raising and influencing them. If you are repressing their ambition, you'll learn in this anthology that you are sitting on a mountain of fortunes that could benefit the entire community, boys and girls, men and women."

Ekari Mbvundula, Creative Director at Story Ink Africa (www.storyinkafrica.com)

Even though the concerns regarding female inclusion and gender equality remain, one thing that remains true is that the inclusion of women is very vital for the shift towards development and poverty eradication. This book, Stories of the Struggle for Education and Equality in Malawi, is a true reflection of what the girl child experiences on ground and I can personally relate to most of these stories. It is clear that once you educate a girl child, you educate the whole nation.

Phyllis Bowazi Manguluti, MBA, PGDEng
Managing Executive Customer Service, Telekom Networks Malawi

In apartheid-era South Africa, a cry rose up from the freedom fighters: "Wathint' abafazi, wathint' imbokodo." You strike a woman, you strike a rock. The women and girls of Malawi are the rocks of their nation. Solid and grounded, they are the foundation upon which families and villages, cities and schools and institutions are built. VoiceFlame helps its participants listen to their own voices and capture that spirit in words on the page, so others can hear these stories and learn to write their own. The determination of these writers to succeed reminds me that when women and girls recognize our own boldness and support one another to secure opportunities for growth and expression, the world is a richer, stronger place. And that's the world I want to live in, ringing out with the voices of women and girls everywhere.

Kimberly Burge, Author, The Born Frees: Writing with the Girls of Gugulethu

Courage and grace are the words that come to me when I reflect on the work of the young African women poets included in this anthology. Not a hint of self-pity permeates their honest expressions, responses to short and simple prompts that served only to nudge their creativity into the open and onto the page. Instead, strength and resilience, hope, humor (humour) and joy shimmer through their poems, reminding me again what a tremendous privilege I was given in the opportunity to facilitate our days of writing together. May the power of their words inspire you, as they do me. And may we cherish the gift of their boldness as they share their words with the world.

Lisa Repko Borden,Certified Amherst Writers & Artists Writing Workshop Leader, and founding partner/co-director of Wema Ventures, a non-profit prioritizing wholistic development in East Africa.

As someone who works with women in the Public Health sector, I believe that education for girls is very important and should be considered a priority in our societies. Now, more than ever, we need more women in the workforce who are educated and skilled to contribute to the development of our nations. Our current education and cultural systems in Malawi have many barriers that girls must surmount to access the best and affordable education. We must continue to challenge the patriarchal status quo in our societies, and believe that women, if given the opportunity, can also 'learn' and 'achieve' anything in life. Thus, I believe the stories in this book are an inspiration to many women out there who are doing everything possible to access education. These stories will also inspire our societies to listen to the voices of women and help them achieve their goals.

James Tayali, Mandela Rhodes Scholar at University of Cape Town,
Studying a Master of Philosophy in Health Innovation.
B.A. in Public Health "17"
University of California, Berkeley

This anthology resonates with my life's journey. It is a must-read book for everyone who hopes to make a difference in their lives, families, communities and around the world. These remarkable stories are loaded with a rare mix of lived experiences in a patriarchal society and how these women defied the odds to obtain education and accomplish their goals. I deeply respect these women for their courage, honesty, love and hope for future generations. Each story is compelling, inspiring, full of insights and will disturb you in the best way.

Nellipher Lewis Mchenga Ph.D., MS, BScN/M, RN

Contents

THE POEMS

ACKNOWLEDGMENTS

Publishing this anthology of Malawi women's voices is a labor of love that would be impossible to accomplish without the bountiful support of friends and family. I want to express my heartfelt gratitude to the special people who accompanied VoiceFlame on this journey toward shining a light on the importance of education for females in Malawi.

First and foremost, I extend my deepest gratitude to the 24 women who volunteered to share their personal stories. You have been relentless in pursuing your education and courageous in telling your stories. You are my inspiration!

Secondly, but no less enthusiastically, many, many thanks to the 28 girls who shared their poetry from the 2019 Voices For Change summer writing camp in Malawi. Your compelling voices are paving the way for those who will stand upon your shoulders. You are young leaders who will have a positive impact on the future of your families, villages and nation.

Thank you to Deborah Nyangulu for graciously writing the foreword to this anthology. Your appetite for education, women's rights and the future of Malawi are immense. I have deep respect for you and your work.

Liz Rogers, the founder of ReGroup Films, thank you for generously volunteering your time and expertise to co-edit, provide the graphic layout and publish this book. I knew from the moment I heard your voice that you were the person to entrust with this project. You are an angel!

Ellie Wood, my dear friend, whose big-hearted donation and compassion for women everywhere, make the purchase and distribution of this anthology in Malawi possible. Your wisdom and support mean the world to me. Thank you.

Katherine Dadachanji, trusted friend and long-time supporter: Your belief in my vision to serve females in Malawi made it possible for the dreams of numerous girls to come true, including my own. You supported the birth of a family of fresh, new voices that will never be forgotten. Many thanks.

Chikondi Lunguzi Njawala, VoiceFlame's Program Manager from 2015 - 2018: Your passion and commitment for mentoring and empowering young girls through writing are commendable, and your contributions to VoiceFlame are immensely appreciated. Many blessings on your continued journey.

Lisa Borden, thank you for offering your expert facilitation skills as an AWA workshop leader for two summer camps in Malawi. Your dedication to enriching lives in Africa is a true gift. I treasure your presence in the world.

My heartfelt gratitude to all the dear friends and donors who provide VoiceFlame, and me in particular, with support through your financial contributions, sponsorships, time, hugs, encouragement, a listening ear and so much more. Your generosity helps to educate and midwife the writing voices of countless girls who will pass it forward to their families, schools and country. You are making an enormous difference in the lives of many.

And to my family who provides me with the unconditional support I need to pursue my dreams: Jim Galinsky, my life partner, my daughter and son-in-law, Amanda and Dave, and the joy in my heart, my grandchildren, Zak and Sadie Lindoerfer. I love you!

Mary Tuchscherer
Executive Director, VoiceFlame

MALAWI

FOREWORD: MORE THAN PATRIARCHY

Deborah Nyangulu

The story of the struggle for education for the girl child in Malawi is one which cannot be separated from how patriarchy is entrenched and resisted in society.

When I was born in the early eighties my parents had long since moved from their respective villages and had made a life for themselves in an urban setting. My father was a senior officer in the Malawian army while my mother was a nurse at the military hospital. My dad was an avid reader and he encouraged all of his children to read. We had a bookshelf in the house and he travelled frequently to foreign lands bringing back books, the latest video cassettes and taped TV shows. When I was five he made sure that I became a member of our local library in the town of Zomba. At that time the library was well stocked and there was a variety of children's books that I could borrow.

I went to a government school for the first part of my primary school and I received a decent education. Judging from both anecdotal and expert evidence, public education standards and public service delivery have since deteriorated marking a sharp contrast between the eighties of the one-party dictatorship and the current democratic dispensation that started in 1994. I do not want to suggest that dictatorship was the right form of government for Malawi, but I mention the point to illustrate that times have changed and the challenges that the Malawi education system faced when I was a school going child are different from those faced by today's children.

The role that patriarchy plays should not be considered the sole limiting factor for girls' access to education. This would be to remain blind to how patriarchy intersects with other dominant factors such as class, bad policies, and colonial legacies to determine opportunities for girls specifically and the Malawian society at large.

In its literal sense, patriarchy refers to rule by fathers and this sense can be exemplified by reference to family headship, where the father is the head of the family and, by extension, his clan. Malawi is, however, a country where both patrilineal and matrilineal lineages exist depending on the ethnic group in question. While ethnicity remains a strong form of both personal and group identification and is usually instrumentalized by those who wield and wish to have political power; the boundaries separating ethnic groups remain fuzzy. Several reasons contribute to this fuzziness: intermarriages, the entrenchment of a classed society that comes with wage labor and urbanization, and a rising nationalist sentiment. These conditions have contributed to shifts in the balance of power such that even in matrilineal societies where fathers traditionally had little say, fathers have now come to the fore as family heads, especially if they are the primary earners of wage labor.

To recognize fathers as family heads is not to condemn them, it is first of all to recognize the role and responsibilities they hold in society. As some of the stories in this anthology attest, the loss of a father can mean the end of education for a girl child. For fathers who take responsibility for their families and send their daughters to school, having a father can potentially be the only thing that guarantees a girl's access to education. If the family is a microcosm of larger societies, then the family is an important clue that can help us ponder the question of access to education for the girl child.

Most of the stories in this anthology engage with the family as the site which determined the trajectory of one's education. Male-headed families notwithstanding, the place of mothers remains key in most of these narratives. Mothers as role models, mothers as wanting better and different futures for their daughters, mothers as friends, mothers as persevering, mothers as resisting patriarchy such as in the case of a mother standing up to an uncle who wants to stop the education of her daughter, mothers as heads of single-headed households -- all these instances affirm the importance of mother-daughter relationships. Had it not been for mothers, most of the women would not have gone far with their education and as one contributor sums it up, "my mother, my anchor."

These instances also affirm that women have agency and do play active roles in their societies. It is therefore not surprising that while most of the contributors recognize the hardships they had to go through to attain their education, they also refuse a victim identity. Reading through the stories one gets a sense that these are women who soldiered on to achieve their dreams and who are unapologetic in demanding their right to education.

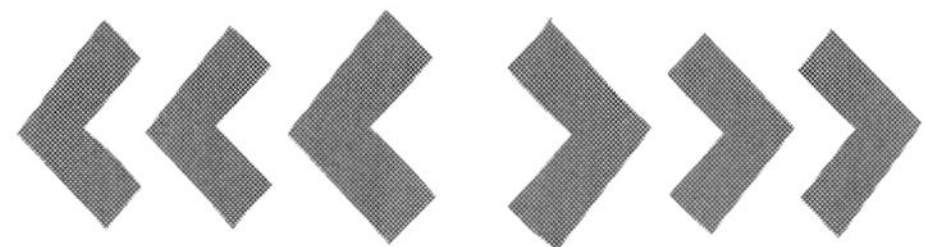

Deborah Nyangulu was born in the city of Zomba located in Southern Malawi. After completing her secondary school education in the Northern city of Mzuzu, she read for a BA in Humanities (English Literatures major) at the University of Malawi. Following successful completion of her BA studies with distinction, Deborah briefly taught English at Our Lady of Wisdom Secondary School. She later joined one of the biggest media companies in Malawi, Blantyre Newspapers, where she worked as a journalist for five years. During her time at Blantyre Newspapers she also ran a weekly column in The Sunday Times. In 2010 Deborah moved to Germany to complete an MA in National and Transnational Studies: Literature, Language and Culture at the University of Muenster.

Following the MA, she enrolled in a PhD program in English Philology at the same university. Her research focuses on the intersections between contemporary African literature and representations of masculinity. She has presented her research at various international academic conferences in Europe and North America. Deborah also works as a lecturer at the University of Muenster and teaches both graduate and postgraduate courses in the fields of African Literature as well as Literary and Cultural Studies.

INTRODUCTION

In Malawi, the struggle for girls to obtain a quality education has many causes, including a lack of ability to pay school fees, gender bias, cultural norms that require girls to perform strenuous domestic chores, and the expectation of early marriage and childbearing. These influences play a significant role in keeping women silent and excluded from reaching their potential.

This challenge is what inspired VoiceFlame to extend a call for submissions inviting Malawi women to tell their stories of overcoming adversity to pursue their education and follow their dreams. VoiceFlame is honored to partner with these 24 women to raise local and global awareness around this pressing issue of providing education for females in Malawi and other nations.

The authors range in age from 17 – 66 years old, and their education levels vary from secondary school to Ph.D's. Some are still at university, while others are active educators, scientists, managers, economists, writers, global leaders and activists. Some of the women were born into what could be considered privileged circumstances by Malawi standards, and

others rose from humble beginnings or extreme poverty. Regardless, they all possess a deep and unwavering hunger to develop themselves through education. Each time I read these stories, I become more inspired by the perseverance, ambition and purpose that guided these women to prevail under unimaginable hardships.

All the stories are unique and yet there are common threads woven throughout the narratives. The importance of having a wise and trusted person in one's life to offer love and support stood out to me as a critical factor on the journey to triumph. Every woman wrote about a mentor, someone who believed in her, who in their own words or actions said, "I see you. You matter. I believe in you."

Mothers, who were often forced to quit school themselves and wanted a better life for their daughters, were highlighted as a primary source of inspiration. Others shared stories of receiving significant encouragement from fathers, step-fathers, teachers, sisters and friends.

Having experienced the warm hearts and generous spirits of many Malawians, I was not surprised to learn that every single woman expressed a sincere desire to pass her hard-earned wisdom forward, to use her gift of education to empower other girls to achieve their dreams. Several of

the authors are already engaged in ambitious projects to create changes in attitudes towards girls and to support those who are motivated to stay in school.

The second section of the book is authored by 28 girls from Mtsiliza Primary School, Chigoneka Community Day Secondary School and Area 49-Gulliver SuperStarz Writing Club who attended the 2018 Voices for Change summer writing camp sponsored by VoiceFlame.

This multi-generational collaboration of essays and poetry weaves together the voices of women who have achieved a level of success through education and young girls who still face the challenges of completing their schooling. These voices fill in empty spaces where once there was silence.

In the Amherst Writers & Artists (AWA) method that VoiceFlame adheres to in all its writing endeavors, we believe that a writer first needs to learn to hear and trust their original voice and understand its value. Once the writer's voice is affirmed, strengthened and listened to, the learning of craft is a natural outgrowth. Therefore, the stories and poems you will read contain minimal edits, honoring the writer's authentic voice.

"The future of our world is only as bright as the future of our girls."
Michelle Obama

THE VOICEFLAME STORY

The magnetism of Malawi aligned itself with my heart from the moment I stepped onto the tarmac and into the alluring breeze that brushed across my cheek, inviting me to accept its warm and hospitable embrace. Now, eleven years later, I recall this instant of knowing that this land and its people had something to offer me and maybe even I had something to contribute to it.

My eyes devoured the bounty of fresh sights and sound on both sides of the well-traveled road as we drove from Kamuza International Airport to Chilambula Lodge, my first resting place in Malawi. Brown men skillfully steered wobbly bicycles with heavy loads of firewood stacked on their heads, overloaded mini-buses swerved and honked around children walking home from school, and young boys sold roasted mice on a stick from the side of the road.

But what truly captivated me were the women wearing colorful chitenjes wrapped around their waists. The vibrant fabric, each piece a work of art, reminded me of fields of fiery sunflowers that grow on the American prairies or patches of orange poppies that dot the California landscape where I live. Others appeared to match the red clay of the earth that absorbed their footsteps. The women's posture was perpendicular to the land – sturdy and upright. Babies hitched to their mother's backs seemed tranquil as they jostled along the hectic roadways. I felt like a bystander watching a New Year's Day parade as we whizzed by in our motorized vehicle.

Who were these women and what type of pain was scorched onto their hearts? What made them laugh or moved them to tears? What secrets lay buried beneath the traditional cloth that adorned their bodies? Were their dreams the same as mine? Could we relate to each other's sorrow and joy? I wanted to know my African sisters, to hear the cadence of their voices as we exchanged stories and inspired each other to speak our truth.

For the next three weeks, I traveled from the capital city of Lilongwe and north to Tukombo Village in Nkhata Bay to absorb every morsel of culture and knowledge about the life of a Malawian woman that I could contain. They welcomed me into their homes and served me warm meals of fresh chambo (my favorite) straight from Lake Malawi, local chicken and rice, cassava greens and nsima. They provided a roof over my head and a soft bed to sleep on. We developed connection and acceptance as we exchanged stories of children, grandchildren, birthing practices, death rituals, domestic violence, dreams of education, menstruation customs and more.

We discovered that we were more alike than different, that we shared common values of compassion, courage and service to others, and that we all wanted the best possible outcomes for our offspring. What separated us was the disparity between the lack of opportunity in a remote African village versus that of an American suburb.

As I continued to witness women's stories, I felt emboldened to take my passion for connecting women through story and writing to a new level. If I could lead writing workshops in America then why couldn't I do it in Malawi? All we needed were pens, paper, a plot of ground to sit on and a willingness to participate.

Before leaving the country, I promised that I would return in eighteen months with eight North American women eager to tell, write and share stories with the women of Malawi. I wanted to build bridges between these two cultures of unique and talented women, and I wanted the resourceful, creative women of Malawi to be seen and heard. I fulfilled my commitment precisely as stated.

What I didn't realize at the time was that the women of Malawi and I were on a parallel journey to reclaim our voices. Together we would assert our freedom to express ourselves, liberating our voices to write and speak our truth even though, at times, we might be terrified.

As a result of our fruitful journey and others that followed, each time with enthusiastic new travelers, I founded VoiceFlame, an international non-profit organization and NGO that supports education, leadership and literacy for girls and women in Malawi. It is an honor to play a small role in shining a light on the voices of Malawian females.

In closing, I want to acknowledge the many disparities in opportunity that exist between the North American women who journey to Malawi and the women we meet in Malawi. The former has far greater access to the freedom to move, to act and to speak openly. It is much more difficult, if not impossible, for most Malawi-born women to travel to the US than it is for Western women to go abroad. It is much simpler for most Western women to have the autonomy to wonder about another woman's story or think about providing a platform for women to write and speak their truth.

VoiceFlame creates an opportunity for connection and advancement out of a belief that all women, regardless of economic status or education should have the chance to use their voices. Stronger, more confident voices lead to better education and better education leads to a healthier society. Perhaps together, through the universal language of story, we can make that a reality.

THE ESSAYS

A Teenage Mother Excels in Biomedical Research

Angeziwa Chunga Chirambo

Angeziwa Chunga Chirambo is a biomedical research scientist affiliated with Malawi Liverpool Wellcome Trust Clinical Research Program and is studying for a PhD with University of Malawi, College of Medicine and University of Liverpool. She is interested in understanding how commensal organisms found in the gastrointestinal tract and its components – specifically Bifidobacteria – controls enteric infections which cause diarrhea in Malawian children.

She is the second child born 35 years ago to a family of 5 children and was raised by a single mother after losing her father at the age of 11. She unfortunately got pregnant when she was in form 2 but managed to go back to school with the support of her mother who seemed to be the only person who believed in her. She successfully finished her secondary education and went on to obtain a bachelor's degree in Environmental Science and Technology (EST) at University of Malawi – The Polytechnic and a master's degree in infectious diseases from London School of Hygiene and Tropical Medicine. She is married, has 3 sons and is studying for a PhD.

Her experience has taught her that life presents different sorts of challenges to all humanity regardless of where you are, but we all have the inherent ability to overcome our own challenges and make our worlds shine with victory. Appreciating the support her mother gave her when she was a teen mother and understanding the challenges faced by other teen mothers, Angeziwa has established the Angeziwa scholarship scheme which supports teen mothers by providing both mentorship and financial support.

Nature defines our early life

I was born on 5 April 1983 at Ngabu Health Centre in what was then the Nsanje District, to a young scientific couple. Baxter Elton Chunga, was an Agricultural scientist and the late Lonely Banda, was a scientist who became a banker. I was the second of 5 children, of whom 4 are still living. I grew up in a family with an average income where all of our basic needs were provided for. My father died when I was 11 years old and we were then raised by a single Christian mother who taught us to have faith in God, encouraged us to work hard in school and excel beyond her level. She unfortunately passed on when I was 18 and though I lost both parents, I gained many others who supported us as a family and made sure we received everything our parents would have wanted for us. Now, more than 20 years after my parents died, I am happily married and have three sons.

Our education and decisions determine our future

My love for science started when I was very young and shaped my life and outlook from an early age. This to a greater extent shaped me as I completed primary education at different schools in north Malawi. I was selected for secondary education (high school level) at Katoto Secondary School (KSS) in Mzuzu and Livingstonia Secondary School in Rumphi by Malawi National Examination Board and Livingstonia Synod respectively. My mother had done part of her senior secondary education at Livingstonia secondary school and the struggles of going to school were still vivid to her when she was looking at secondary schools, so she decided that I should go to KSS. After passing my final secondary exams, I was selected to go to University of Malawi, The Polytechnic to study Environmental Science and Technology (EST) where I majored in Environmental Management. In 2016, I was awarded a master's degree in Infectious Diseases by the London School of Hygiene and Tropical Medicine. This was funded by the Commonwealth Scholarship Commission (CSC) and the Malawi Liverpool Wellcome Trust Clinical Research Programme (MLW). In 2017, MLW and CSC awarded me a grant to study for a PhD in Gastrointestinal Infections. Through this grant, I am investigating how normal flora (gut microbiota) and Bifidobacteria (the most predominant member of the gut microbiota in breast-fed children) help to protect Malawian children against enteric infections, with an aim of developing gut microbiota derived therapeutic agents that can control diarrhea infections in Sub Saharan African children.

Life is full of challenges

I lost my father when I was quite young and could not understand much of what was going on. It was however quite hard as we had to move from the suburbs to denser communities. This meant going to cheaper local schools as opposed to expensive schools that were providing high quality education. I had really wanted to go to Mary Mount private Secondary School but did not want to ask my mother to send me there as I knew she already had a lot on her plate. I therefore made use of the opportunities that were available to me. Losing my mother was the most painful thing that has happened in my life. She was at the core of my life, was and still is my model. My life would not have been what it is without her.

Motherhood at 17

Motherhood is a significant and important aspect of life for most women worldwide, yet for women in Malawi, a community where motherhood is highly regarded, motherhood is considered crucial to a woman's identity. Motherhood brings value and respect to women. This is however not the case when you get pregnant when you are only 17 and still in school. In a twinkling of an eye, I had to start thinking and behaving as a mother to be, a grown-up person. This was very hard and was as though one day I am a girl playing fulaye (local netball kind of game) with my friends and barely a month later, I am not expected to do that. Neither am I expected to be chatting with those friends. I am supposed to change friends. My friends should now be mothers and most of these were married ladies who were much older than me. I am now going to be a mother. This was a result of a single sexual encounter with a person I believed to have loved and shared dreams with me, yet even he could not express the same love he professed before the sexual encounter.

My joy and my dreams were shattered. I was young and so naïve, still enjoying childhood with my peers and all of a sudden, things turned around. I lost most of my girlfriends because they did not want to associate with me and neither would their parents recommend. I ended up hanging in between being a girl who could still play fulaye and a mother who also had to think of the child apart from herself.

This becomes even more complicated for most girls when their family also decides to abandon them. I was very fortunate to have a loving and supporting mother who sacrificed her dignity just for me. In my community people regard a mother who supports a girl in such a situation, as the one who was and is encouraging the girl to be sleeping around. When all the community around you, family, friends and neighbors look at you as a prostitute and you are on the front page of the local news, your world threatens to crumble around you and you have every reason to give up on everything. Your life is filled with shame and embarrassment. I am pregnant, yes. I am the hot news for the bad thing, yes. I have ruined my education, yes. I have brought shame to my family, yes. What next?

Will this be the end of my life, my dreams and my future? I accepted my fate but then became encouraged and told myself that this would not be the end of me. I would go through whatever form of pain and hardship that this will bring to me, but will come through it as the victor.

A plan for the new path that my life was going to take had to be written down, a plan that I was determined to follow. I accepted that I would stay home for one year to take care of my baby, but then went back to finish secondary school. I had always dreamt of having a bachelor's degree from the University of Malawi but at this time I decided that I will not only attain a bachelor's degree but also a Master's. I had not even heard of let alone dreamt of studying for a PhD. In my plan, marriage would come at a time when I was independent and financially stable, when I was working after getting my first degree. I was going to get married to someone who could be my partner in all aspects and not because of the financial support.

Gender based challenges

There are several challenges that I have come across in my pursuits just because I am a woman. This is aggravated by the fact that I am in the scientific field which is mostly regarded to be for men. Being a teenage mother brings with it challenges and negative stereotype that can seem to be carried for life. While a teen mother stays home for a year or more and tries to balance her career and be a young mother, the father of the child is moving on with his dreams since he is neither expelled from school nor in most cases held responsible for the day to day life of the child.

We have the power to overcome

My life story is about an orphaned girl who got pregnant in secondary school but still moved on to achieve her dreams. The big question could be, how did I manage to do it? I could say there are about three or four principles that helped me to overcome.

First of all, in all the challenges I face, I have learnt to accept them. We have the power to influence what happens today and tomorrow but what has already happened cannot be changed. I can't bring back my parents from the grave and I cannot take away the pregnancy. I accepted that I cannot live with the same lifestyle of the kids of rich people. When I was 17 I made a decision to accept that this is my child, I am now a mother and therefore had to accept that responsibility.

Second, I had to re-align my life. I had dreamt of becoming a scientist when I was very young, but I was not prepared for some of the obstacles that came my way. I had to make a new plan for my life, focusing on the goal while avoiding all the temporal, fake glittering gold that the world provides. Having a plan was not enough, but my determination to achieve my dreams took me through every single day for I had to show myself and the world that I "am more than my scars" (Andrew Davidson).

Having people that you can look up to and those that can support you greatly influences the progress you make. As Oliver Goldsmith said, "People seldom improve when they have no other role model but themselves to copy." I had and still have role models, both male and female. These are people that challenged me and I wanted to be an achiever like them. The people that have significantly contributed to my progress in life have mostly been ladies but unfortunately only one of them was Malawian, nor did I have a role model who was a teenage mother who could understand and support me. I accepted this and found people around me whom I could look up to.

More important is that the hand of God has held me every step of the way. In the valleys and on the mountains, He has always been there. When

I am about to give up, He reminds me that, with Him by my side, I can do it. His arms have always been available to give me a warm embrace.

We do not give up but continue dreaming big

Academically, I would like to finish my PhD, become a junior then senior researcher and ultimately establish a research group that will employ other scientists to study ways of controlling enteric infections in Malawian children by using probiotics and not antibiotics.

More importantly, I desire to continue supporting as many girls as I can in achieving their dreams. I'd like to help prevent teenage pregnancies but also support those who do get pregnant while young, especially the disadvantaged girls in rural Malawi. This I hope to do by providing mentorship, moral and financial support.

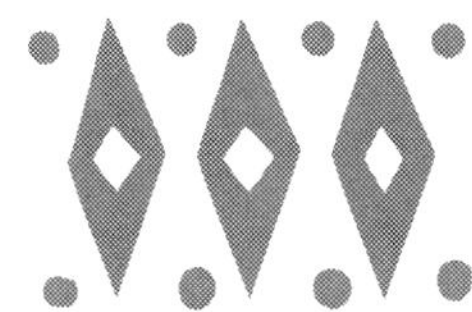

Amake Naomi (Naomi's Mother)

Naomi Kaleso Kanzangaza

Naomi Kaleso Kanzangaza was born on 12 December 1977 in Malawi, the first born and only daughter in a family of five children. She is a wife and the mother of two children, Nathan and Chloe and lives in Lilongwe, Malawi. She holds an advanced diploma in Information Technology obtained in 2002 from University of Malawi Polytechnic and has worked in different organisations in Malawi as well as the United Kingdom.

Her current job is far different from what she learned in school. She is working as an assistant to an executive in a Telecommunication Company. What she loves about her job is that she gets to organise the details of the high flying life of her boss, her travels in and out of Malawi, her accommodation bookings and meetings and she gets to be exposed to many people along the way. She loves organising things.

Naomi has lived in and out of Malawi both as a child and as an adult. In 1986 TO 1987, she lived with her parents and two brothers in Scotland, UK. From 1995 to 1998, she lived in Tanzania, East Africa and from 2003 to 2007 in Manchester, UK. She also visited Kenya, Zambia, Zimbabwe, Botswana, South Africa, Mozambique, Holland and Germany.

Her joy in life apart from spending time with her family is travelling, appreciating different ways of life and beautiful scenery, books, cooking and watching the occasional movie.

Naomi's passion is to encourage others, especially women, to be educated, to be well read and exposed which in turn make them confident at heart.Her dream is to see an Africa that makes children's education a priority, especially to the girl child, and affords opportunities equally to girls as well as boys.

Mummy grew up in a family of seven and went to primary school up to standard eight. While in standard eight, her father told her to get married to a young man who was at the time in secondary school. She did not have a choice in the matter. She got engaged and had her first child at the age of 16.

I was born when she was 18, the second born in a family of six and the only girl among males. My mother was very excited. By this time my father had finished high school, gone to Theological College and became a church minister in a village in Thyolo.

Life was very hard for them. However, by a sheer stroke of luck my father was selected to go to the U.K. for extra studies for two years. He went, leaving the family behind. Coming back after two years he was transferred to a church in town.

As years went by, my mother began to see that there is a place for education in a woman's life, especially because again and again foreigners would come to socialise with the family and as such, language became a problem.. When I was eight years old my father was again gone to Scotland on a scholarship. After he started on his studies, the sponsors there agreed to bring his family to Scotland too. My mum was assisted with processing passports, yellow fever books and everything else that was necessary. Then the departure day came.

The first leg of the journey was from Blantyre to Lilongwe. This was okay because everyone spoke in Malawi's mother tongue, but from Lilongwe we landed in Kenya. Because it was mummy's first time to travel and she was not fluent in English, it began to pose big problems for her. As luck would have it, she latched on to a Reverend who assisted her in finding the correct terminal. From Kenya we landed in Amsterdam and here, it was just too much. The accent was something else, no English and with three kids in tow.

We missed our flight to Scotland. As the voice beamed over the intercom, mum could not make head or tail of it, she began to go this way and that way, and when she arrived at the counters for help she could not explain herself. We were stranded for a long while until eventually she could make out her name being called, went to the counters and we were finally put on another flight. We managed to arrive, but very late.

This day pained my mother greatly and opened up her eyes. On this day, she swore that her daughter would never drop out of school early for marriage or whatever. She swore she would make everything possible for her daughter to get a decent education.

After her stay in Scotland, she became a crusader for girls education in her village and started with me. She would wake me up early, get me ready and send me running to the local school, which was a thirty minute walk from our house. After school, she would check my books, see what I learned, make me write homework and scold me for the bits I did not do well.

Repeatedly, she would remind me how she had messed her life up by marrying early and how she did not want that pattern repeated in my life.

When I had finished primary six, she persuaded my father to send me to a Catholic boarding school. At this point my parents relatives began to pressure my mother saying, "Why are you stressing the girl? She is ripe for marriage. She should marry and raise children."

Pressure began to mount on my mother and also on me. Fellow friends of my age began to drop out of school and get married. I would hear stories of so-so has given birth to a child. I was around twelve at the time and most of the girls I knew were around that age, and not more than fifteen.

My mother did not bow to pressure. Her story was still the same. Work hard. Get an education. Live differently. So I went to boarding school, more to take me away from the mindset of my many relations and school mates who were encouraging early marriage. I did my primary seven and eight and was selected to go to secondary school.

I met a boy in my first year of secondary school and he became my boyfriend. When my mother heard about it ooh she was outraged. Her fear was I would be seduced into early sex and drop out from school because of pregnancy She was right. That was the trend at the time in most secondary schools, so I ended it and got back to studying without distractions.

Mother kept on pushing me and nagging me. I finished form four, passed well but in 1996, it was not easy to get into university. The numbers taken in were few and I did not make it. She was as devastated as I was. I could have given up at this time and gone home defeated, but not so.

At this time, my father was working in East Africa. My mum encouraged me to enroll in college where I did an Information Technology Diploma. Four years later I went to University of Malawi Polytechnic and did An Advanced Diploma in Information Technology.

From there I have worked in several companies in Malawi and abroad. Currently I am working for TNM. I am a wife and a mother of two, a boy and a girl. My mother went on to help even pay school fees for several girls in her village and still encourages many using her story as an example for why education is important to girls as well as boys.

She is turning 60 in 2018 and her message is still the same. "Get an education. Get an education. Education takes you far and gives you confidence and boldness, especially for the girl child. Marriage can wait, add value to yourself first," she says. She means it from the heart.

Over the years, my father found an English teacher for her and I bought her many English books. She has upgraded herself to the extent that she can carry an English conversation for hours.

She is my model. I love her. I have the message in my heart too so my daughter will have no escape. She will get this message at home, that education is key. Before grandma comes and starts on her, I will have done my work.

In this generation, more than in past generations, we cannot escape this fact. Education is very important. In societies that do not consider girls important, it must be known that girls can study too, become independent, and not have to marry as a way of survival. I learned it from my own Mum, after she discovered how crucial it is, the hard way. My mum Esme Mkwate.

Today I meet a lot of those girls who dropped out from school, getting married early. They are saddled with children who they are failing to support properly and educate, and many of them have been divorced and their life is miserable.

Having travelled in Europe and certain parts of Africa I agree with her. She is right.

My goal is to go back to University and do a Master's in Business Administration and then start my own businesses which will afford me enough free time to lobby and join causes that empower girls education.

Let Her Be!

Mrs. Bertha Simbeye Chiudza

Bertha Simbeye Chiudza is a leader, the mother of two beautiful and brilliant girls, Hannah and Hellen. She is a Christian, a feminist and gender justice advocate, is passionate about women's and girls' rights and social justice. She is currently the Gender Mainstreaming Coordinator for United Nations Office for Project Services (UNOPS) based in Copenhagen, Denmark. Previously, she worked with Oxfam in Malawi as the Women's Rights Program Manager. She has also worked with organizations such as UNFPA as the National Program Professional on the Gender Equality and Women Empowerment Program, UN WFP as the Gender Advisor, Plan International as the Child Protection Coordinator and with local Civil Society Organizations; the Centre for Human Rights and Rehabilitation and the Society for the Advancement of Women.

Bertha was the first Malawian intern to be selected for Nigeria's CLEEN Foundation program on the Role of Civil Society on Access to Justice and Police Reform in Africa in 2009. She is also the first Malawian who was awarded the University College of London, Institute of Education Centenary Scholarship in 2010. Bertha holds a Master of Arts Degree in Education, Gender and International Development from UCL, Institute of Education and Bachelor of Arts Degree in Biblical Studies and Education from the African Bible College, Lilongwe, Malawi.

In 2004 during the World AIDS Day, Bertha was awarded Third Best Essay Writer on 'Safer Choices on HIV and AIDS Prevention among the Youth' by the Eastern and Southern Health Community in Africa and conferred by the late President of the Republic of Malawi, H.E. Bingu wa Muntharika. Bertha serves on a number of Boards including Action Aid International, Malawi office. Bertha loves nature, traveling and discovering new places, reading people's biographies and inspirational books, writing and sporting activities.

"Let her be!"

"You are not supposed to talk like that as a girl!"

"No, you should not question why this boy is treated differently from you!"

"No, no, no, no, why are you playing soccer with the boys? Go and play netball, that is for the girls!"

"You smile too much, you deliberately attract men to you with the way you smile, please try not to smile as such!"

"We cannot allow you to stand in front of us (male chiefs), that is not allowed in this community, if you think you are learned enough with your western culture of gender, that cannot happen in this community."

Those were some of the many voices I heard growing up as a young girl, and it seemed normal as many would tell me, "That is the way things are, they will never change." But the voice that stood up most and challenged all these stereotypes and social norms was that of my dad, "Let her be who she wants to be."

Growing up in a middle-income family and low density suburb, I wouldn't say that life was very tough for me, it was rather nice as both of my parents were working as civil servants in the education sector. We didn't have plenty, but our parents instilled in us the spirit of contentment and sharing the little we would have. I grew up in a family of eight children (five girls and three boys) and other relations who also formed part of the Simbeye's family. That taught me a lot about coexistence, tolerance and compromise.

While I was growing up, there were some norms that kept me wondering and questioning why things were done as they were. Sometimes I would not publicly question, for fear of repercussions and I would somehow think that something was wrong with me for thinking differently. I noted that many people who surrounded me would not question or raise those issues either in public or in private.

I remember very well when I was in primary school, two (female and male) teachers doing inspection of classrooms found that our classroom wasn't swept and mopped. Upon noting that, they both had to summon all of us girls to the front of the classroom and whipped us for not making the classroom tidy and the boys laughed at us. After the girls went through the corporal punishment, the boys were told to step outside the classroom and wait for us girls to clean the classroom.

I was boiling and wondering why we had to be treated as such because we are girls. Later that day, I asked my female teacher why things are this way, the response from her was, "Bertha, you are a girl, things will always be like that for you girls, this is your responsibility as girls and it will never change. You ask too many questions and you are stubborn these days as if you are a boy. By the way, I don't want to see you playing soccer with boys again, you have to be at the girl's netball field not there, do you understand?"

I could not really respond to some of those sentiments, but I kept asking myself that why should I try to fit in when I don't want to. Surviving different forms of violence both during my early years and high school life made me toughen my skin and not normalize what seemed to be the bad behaviors and attitudes towards me and my fellow girls.

Transitioning into secondary school had its own challenges especially with regards to my femininity and peer pressures. Several times I was told by teachers that I was too welcoming to people with my smile and that was not a good sign and men could take advantage of me. "You smile too much Bertha, you deliberately attract men to you with the way you smile, please try not to smile like that...your smile sends different signals, it is as if you are seducing men!" I remember one female teacher calling me in the teacher's staff room and saying to me in front of other teachers, "If one day you find yourself surviving some form of sexual violence, you will have to blame yourself, not the boys or the men." My heart broke, I tried few times sitting in front of the mirror when no one was watching, rehearsing how not to smile, but I failed. I told myself that I can't change, I just have to be me and never blame myself for that.

The do's and don'ts were the order of the day growing up as a girl. In my pursuit of serving the communities in Malawi when I had just started doing community development work, I went to a certain area. I was well dressed in my view. I had a head wrapper, a long dress with long sleeves and had put on top of the dress a wrapper. I looked at myself in the mirror that morning, happy and told myself, "You are really dressed very well and the community will accept you. Bear the very hot weather for the sake of being accepted and accomplish that which you have been sent there for." I smiled and off I went full of energy, but upon arrival and meeting with the community elders, one of them asked me, "You have come with who madam?" I answered, "It is me and the driver (male)."

Looking surprised, he said, "So is it you, we were told that you are coming from your office to facilitate this session or you are waiting for your colleagues to come?" Before I could respond that indeed it was me, he had posed yet another question, "Or maybe it is the driver who will address us?" When I had responded that they should not expect anyone else from the office apart from me, I was told point blank, "We cannot allow you as a woman to stand in front of us (male chiefs and community opinion leaders). That is not allowed in this community, if you think you are learned enough with your western thinking of gender, that cannot happen in this community. You better go back young lady or come here only when you have your male colleagues who would ably come and address us."

I was baffled, cried inside of me and couldn't believe what I had just encountered. His voice kept ringing in my ears as we drove back, yet it was also a huge motivation for me to forge ahead and never give up on my passion. That encounter didn't make me throw in a towel, it made me go back to the drawing board, re-strategize, re-think and re-engage that community with other strategies.

Fast forward to ten years later, it is the very same community leader, very resistant to change then, who is now one of the champions for women's rights and gender justice who keeps telling my story to his fellow leaders. A few years ago he told me, "I like your focus and determination Bertha, you don't give up easily."

While pursuing my first degree, it was yet another ride of life challenges, but for purposes of this article, I would choose to write about the hurdles I encountered in primary and secondary school as I believe those are the very critical stages that could have made me or broken me, and that could eventually affect my career path.

My love for writing grew while I was in college. It was and is still therapeutic and self-motivating. Following my dreams through education as I was pursuing my first and second degrees, I knew exactly what I wanted to do in life, work for women's rights, gender justice and that wasn't going to change no matter the various opposition I got. I have had cases where some people would even want me to justify why I was so interested in gender justice related work. "What really happened to you that makes you so passionate about gender and women's rights issues?" This, insinuating that the kind of profession I was getting in is only for the people, especially women who have failed relationships, or hate men, or even those who are not 'Christian' enough. I tell people that no one will stop me from being me or from doing what I am passionate about and neither will I do so to them. Different passion, different calling, different paths and different vision and all along I have chosen which battles are worth my energy to fight for and which ones are not and, this has kept me going.

The environment I grew up in made me want to quit at times, as I somehow thought that something was wrong with me. But, my family, mom, dad, siblings, partner, friends played a very big role in helping me through the processes and realize my dreams. My dad, Mr. E.K. Simbeye kept telling me, "Be the Bertha you want to become, follow your dreams and never give up on those dreams and what God has placed on your heart." That has kept me going and fighting on.

One thing I keep telling parents and guardians in all the spaces I find myself in is to help their children be who they want to become. What is laid on their heart may seem unusual to them as parents, but as the main duty bearer for these children, they need to help them to realize their dreams. Speak well about your children. Wish them well, encourage them and support them in their education or any other life pursuits they may have.

To the many girls of my motherland, I say, "Keep shining, as you will have to decide for yourself first what you want to do in life. Exercise your agency, be you and don't let the world determine the world for you. It doesn't matter how many times you get knocked down. All that matters is that you get up one more time than you were knocked down."

Have I achieved my life goals yet? I have some, while some I haven't, but I am getting there, and I always say the time I will depart on this earth, I will leave a very happy and accomplished woman for my country. I do take my success in life from the impact I have made on the many girls, women and other vulnerable groups of people and never have I regretted that.

My ultimate goal and vision in life is to see a society that is gender just, a society where equal opportunities are given to girls, boys, women, men. A Malawi free from gender-based violence and with equitable development, free from poverty and inequalities.

Motivation by Deprivation

Catherine Ndiwo Banda

Catherine Ndiwo Banda is a Lecturer in the Christian Education Department at African Bible College in Lilongwe, Malawi. A PhD candidate in education from the University of Malawi, Chancellor College, she also earned a Master of Arts in Christian Education from Africa International University in Nairobi, Kenya and a B.A. in Biblical Studies with a minor in Christian Education from African Bible College in Lilongwe, Malawi.

I was born in a well-to-do family by Malawian standards. My father had a rare occupation in my community as he was a primary school teacher as well as a successful businessman. He started with a small business which grew to two large shops along with houses and cars. He would have been labeled affluent in the time we were growing up and in primary school. My mother was a housewife, a businesswoman alongside my father - and a school dropout. Yet, despite her lack of formal education, mother was rich in both cultural experiences and problem-solving skills.

My mother was born the first of four daughters. Her father, my grandfather, was a chief and according to Ngoni culture, was to be succeeded by his first-born son. As he'd had no sons, he groomed my mother to take his position one day. He would invite the girls to attend village courts where disputes were settled and could delegate things to them. He raised his daughters with a heavy hand, so they would be strong both physically and mentally, reminding them that as chiefs they were not to be weak-minded.

Like most men in his culture, my grandfather spent his money and resources on beer, ignoring his responsibility to educate his daughters. However, an uncle, rich by village standards, assumed the responsibility neglected by my grandfather and sent my mother and her sisters to school. My mother went up to class six before the uncle died. His death deprived my mother and her sisters of school fees and they all dropped out of school.

My father was a teacher at the school during this time and needed a wife. Rather than sponsor her education, he offered to marry her, and it was from this circumstance that I along with my eleven siblings, were born.

Twelve children, seven boys and five girls. The first and second born were girls followed by a mixture of boys and girls with the last five born being boys. My parents are Ngonis, a tribe who follow a patrilineal family system. I learned from my grandparents that the Ngonis were a warlike tribe that came from South Africa and fought their way to Malawi where they are currently settled. Their warlike nature acknowledged only male power, as only men went to war while women were left in camps to do domestic work. The men in my tribe were and still are more powerful than women in many aspects of life.

Learned gender roles and denial of opportunities for women play a major role in enhancing male domination and women in my tribe were denied the opportunity of both public and private decision making. Decisions were made by men, with occasional exceptions for women from royal families of chiefs. My mother was privileged to have been born in the lineage of chiefs and the fact that my grandfather had no sons worked to the advantage of my mother and her sisters. Being born in a family without sons around gave my mother and her sisters a rare opportunity to participate in decisions both publicly and privately. My grandfather urged his daughters "to behave like boys" because they never had a brother "to rely upon." They were allowed to be present while my grandfather was settling disputes. He did not want his daughters to suffer for lack of knowledge of the historical background in matters of the village. For this reason, my mother grew to be independent and taught her sons and daughters to be independent in decision making. I call her experience "empowerment by default."

My father grew up with his mother, as his father had gone to South Africa for work and had never returned. His mother had the tradition that men alone were decision makers and, as a result, my father, the first born in his family, was the decision maker for the entire family, including his mother.

This tradition carried forward to my parent's home, my father wanting to empower my brothers, more than my sisters and I, in decision making.

Although my father was educated to the level of a primary school teacher, his view of the relationship between men and women, boys and girls did not change. The school curriculum of his time did not include social studies nor were gender issues taught as part of any subject. Yet, gender issues and traditions were taught as "unintended curriculum" in school. Teachers brought with them their attitudes and opinions, therefore school played a major role, encouraging boys to be the decision makers and not girls.

The transfer of property to one's offspring is another area in which men are more powerful than women in my tribe where traditionally, a woman leaves her parents and lives with her husband in his village. The patrilocal residential pattern is followed closely and because girls are expected to leave the village once they get married, girl children are not considered worthy except for the dowry they bring with them. Men exercise complete control over wealth and earnings and pass on their property to their male children. Women have little power in any decision to do with wealth and although women do not possess wealth, they are relied upon to earn it.

Malawi's economy is agriculturally based, and women work equally with men in their fields but must also handle domestic workloads that include cooking, washing, caring for children, the sick and the elderly, fetching water and firewood and often tending smaller animals such as goats and pigs. Failure to do these household chores has led to physical violence and although men and women work in the same manner to produce wealth, women do not benefit as much as men from the wealth and are oppressed economically.

My father also believed that wealth belonged to the father and his sons. He loved all of his children, yet when he thought of heirs to his property, male children had rights that the females did not. This mind-set was evident in our family as we were growing up and he sent both girls and boys to school, but for different reasons. Girls were sent to school so that they would not have to beg him and their brothers for resources but would earn their own money from employment. He believed that no man would claim his daughter's salary as his money, therefore his daughters would be safe economically. He believed that his daughters would not have to do the heavy workload required of girls in the villages. Boys were encouraged to go to school so that they would be able to take over his businesses successfully and he would often take his sons with him when he would run errands after school. Daughters were never invited.

When he acquired his first vehicle, he taught my fourteen-year-old brother to drive while my mother and the older sisters were present. Although my brother was under and age unable to drive legally, my father allowed this while his daughters of legal age were deprived of this opportunity. The signs on my father's shops said, "M. M. Mbeya and Sons" making certain that we girls were not counted as heirs to his wealth. This show of discrimination and deprivation acted as a motivation to my older sisters and one by one they started going to secondary school and beyond with their education. My mother was determined that not being able to finish her education would not happen to her daughters and encouraged us saying, "It is unfortunate that I did not finish my education. But for you my daughters, you have all that it takes for one to be educated. As for wealth, do not worry as school is the most important wealth a person can have."

Men are more powerful than women in my tribe because of patriarchy and dominate because of socialization. When a man, or even a young boy does something wrong he is understood and forgiven faster than a woman or a girl committing the same wrong. Unfortunately, this behavior is perpetuated by fellow women or girls whether they have been to school or not.

As I was growing up, school was no better than home in terms of inequalities. In my primary school years, I struggled with teachers who used to refer to boys as the standard for achievement. When announcing results of exams if a girl did better than boys, most teachers would state "Mtsikana amene wachita chamuna ndi…" meaning "the girl who has performed like a man is…." This made most girls feel as though they were gaining in performance but that boys were still better or were supposed to be better than the girls. For the boys who did well, the teacher would announce their names without further comment.

In secondary school we were compared to boys from a neighboring secondary school with statements like, "boys cannot fail the way you have done," often heard when teachers were angry with our performance. Whenever I heard boys being elevated in my presence I would wonder what was special with them. I would try as much as possible to beat them in performance in order to be like them. I had learned from my mother that every child is capable of achieving great things with hard work and determination. What I heard from teachers was very different. I forgive them as this was before the idea of equality was taught, even to teachers.

Girls, in the face of discouragement, discrimination, oppression and deprivation you can choose to be positive in every aspect of your life. Remember, you are responsible for your life. You have nobody to blame. Your environment may be harsh but how you react to it all depends on you and you alone. The boys in my family who were cherished so much by father ended up as spoiled and irresponsible children after which my father realized his mistakes and removed "and Sons" on his shops. He loves his children equally.

It Must Come to an End

Cecilia Haleke

Cecilia Haleke is twenty-two years old and is currently in her third year at the Polytechnic studying for her Bachelor of Arts in Journalism. She was born in Mzimba, on 24 November 1995. She was the fourth born in a family of eight, two brothers and six sisters. She started her primary school education at Namasoko FP School in Phalombe, her home district, TA Mnkhumba. In 2004, Cecilia's family moved to Balaka, where she did her standard three and four and wrote her Primary School Leaving Certificate Examination at Ngwangwa LEA in 2009. She attended her secondary education at Andiamo Private Secondary in Balaka and wrote her MSCE in 2013. She started writing when she graduated from secondary school and was waiting for her UNIMA entrance examination. She was inspired by the novels she enjoyed reading written by female authors so much that she started writing her own life stories. Cecilia wanted to tell someone about them but couldn't because of pride. In time, the paper became the best friend she could share any story with.

The market place was more like a playground to me, I could hardly let a day pass without going there after school. I liked helping my parents in their business. A lot of customers called me the "clever one." I wondered why you would call a child clever when she just says the same things her parents say when negotiating in business? I was nine, a junior in primary school and had just moved to Balaka from our home district Phalombe. I also wondered why can't I just be a buyer like these people one day, without having to call for customers, "tomatoes 10, 20, onions 5, 10!"

I started wondering each day when I was at the market and the colourful, smart clothes some lady customers wore always dragged my attention away from other customers. The shiny nail-like shoes that shaped their fine movement shook a lot of dreams in me and was driving me away from the dark unpromising village life that I originally thought was fun and pleasant.

The big kachere tree close to aunt Lekeleni's house was our 'after supper' gathering area. The shiny stars and bright moon called on all the children around the Nkhoma tribe, of course not to play under the tree but rather along the sandy road up Chinguma Hill. We showered in that sand before bed.

"Achiphwedeeeeeeyayeee!" We would hear aunt Lekeleni's husband shout. He was a drunkard and referred to my younger sister Susan by achiphwede, meaning "fat one,“ as she was the fattest kid among us. "Kwatelerera, eyayee, kumtundako" which means, "situation is hot and exciting up there," we would all respond. Some running towards him to get his bicycle. Others making a fire, so we would sit around and sing with him until elder siblings decide it was time to sleep. He helped us end our days with fun moments, forgetting how unpleasantly we started each day.

Namasoko FP School was named after our village and we covered less than half a kilometre to school, except for the days when we took the mountain paths on our way back for fruits. It was fun. My father worked as a driver for one of the big men in the area, a job that barely helped him support a wife and 7 children. Mother was known for her expertise in clay pottery, and so was her business. Subsistence farming added a little for our table.

Problems ripened when three of my elder siblings got selected to Mpasa, a Community Day Secondary (CDSS) which was every primary school student's dream. My family decided to move to Balaka for business, leaving the ones in secondary school back in the village. We lived at my uncle's house for three months before we could manage to rent our own house.

Settling in town became frustrating. The changes in lifestyle and social life proved difficult to adapt to. The free water in the village was sold here and the house here we have to pay rent for, as opposed to free land given by chiefs, where a simple grass thatched house, that called for a new roof every year, is built. There was the school fund each pupil had to pay, when I thought primary education is free in this country? The fish business my father started failed to generate money for all these costs. It makes me laugh today that we had to stay home for two weeks or so because of K150 per term.

The only drama was the thought of sitting under a tree, with a black board leaning against it and calling it 'our' classroom at Balaka Primary. Our attention being distracted by pupils screaming when ants tasted a bit of their skin. I got to count the number of cars passing on the road behind our so-called classroom, as is expected of a villager in town. At Namasoko, I would worry about bringing buckets of water and clay to recover the floor but not the winds which kept showering us with sand here. I easily got distracted when I heard or saw something about town kids that was never seen in our village world. A nice dress or shoe, even the language which was different from my Lomwe accent, over which others would laugh at me. And, my academic performance was very poor.

The business started boosting. There were now a lot of commodities like beans, rice, cooking oil, Irish potatoes, and all kinds of spices in addition to the tomatoes and onions. By the time I was in standard five, our family had adapted to the new environment and my parents got us transferred to Ngwangwa Primary.

The conditions were much better there, the school had good classrooms and my desires for a better life increased. I started working hard and my performance improved to average but I wanted more. The grades that would make me recognized were not so easy. The battle reached its peak in standard eight. Those familiar with primary life may agree that we studied hard to beat others, not necessarily for one's own good. I never got to be on position one, however I was in the top five in mock examination.

In the third term, I stopped spending my afternoons at the market and dedicated that time to memorizing things because to call it studying is a bit much. We had beautiful classrooms, beautiful school uniforms, few pupils, but little experience. I should have stayed at Balaka Primary. Our class was the first to sit for Primary School Leaving Certificate Examination (PLSCE).

I had already started my secondary education at Andiamo Private, the new school when the results were released. I was selected to St. Louis Montfort CDSS. I had been told "It runs in the family," and I was proud, not because I wanted St. Louis, but because I was the only girl among the only four who were selected from our school.

Both I and my parents preferred Andiamo to St. Louis, the boarding school. I started so well and the Italian volunteer teacher Anna Dahl awarded me with a sponsorship after the very first term. My life drastically changed because of that hero. My parents forgot worrying about school fees, yet I hardly survived. The business had started declining, with lots of people entering the market and I wasn't the only child my parents had to think of. Boarding school life was frustrating.

I still remember the four basic needs that made up my whole budget for each term: sugar, washing and bath soap and body lotion. Each day started with admirations, the nice school shoes my friends wore, the porridge additives I never bought, the tea I missed some days on break because I could not buy bread or anything to take with me, the way I relied on kitchen relish when I couldn't afford the relish that was being sold, and each time I was hungry, counting down time for the kitchen bell to ring.

One teacher kept saying, "If you are not good in some area, try your best in another," and so I tried my best academically which was fruitful. I was the one student every teacher liked, as did the administration, so school materials were never in my budget. I received every year's best academic performer award and was so famous at school. I wrote my MSCE in 2013 and surprisingly, when I go there these days, some students are familiar with my name. Maybe not because my performance was delightful, but what happened after that.

I was chatting with two of my best friends one afternoon alongside the M1 road where one of them was selling nuts and the other one read, "… and the first ambassador to represent Andiamo Secondary in the University of Malawi is Cecilia Haleke…" It was a Facebook status on the Director of Schools' timeline. "She has been selected to study Bachelor of Arts in Journalism at the Polytechnic," he continued, wondering if I had really applied for that program because I loved science. Journalism was my first choice indeed though it was never my dream, I just didn't want to be left out. The next time you see your friend abandoning you, don't get surprised much, and rather consider their reason for doing that. I heard the message and jumped with excitement. I left them and ran home to find only the chickens waiting, so I shared the news first with them.

My parents came after I had prepared the evening meal and I recall a basket of tomatoes falling from my mother's head after hearing the news. She shouted "Cecilia!" as she always does when I do something she did not expect.

The director of schools and the Andiamo family found me another Italian sponsor for my tertiary education as an award. I was the only student from our school selected to university. I realized that the "runs in the family" statement I rebelled against could be proven wrong. I decided to bring change to my own life and so to my family. I started re-branding the Cecilia people knew into the one that should be admired like the ladies at the market, perhaps even more admirable.

This feeling was firmly implanted in me on the day I was leaving for university. I was sitting in the back-corner seat, my earphones on, listening to Skeffa Chimoto's song Ali Mbali Yanga (The Lord is On My Side). We were still in the depot and I looked through the window at the muddy road along the depot's fence. I saw my father sitting on those big sacks of cabbages, onions and Irish potatoes, with baskets of tomatoes on the other side of the lorry. I knew he risked his life sitting on that.

"It must come to an end," I whispered.

We Are Each Other's Keeper

Chikondi Lunguzi Njawala

We are each other's keeper
Keeper of each other's hearts
Free to share
Feelings from inner most being.

We are able to surrender
Surrender our thoughts and fears
Our griefs and fears.

All seems perfect in people's eyes
Even though all is not well
We have each other's back
We hold each other's hands
And carry on as normal
For we are each other's keeper.

As I Leave Here

Chikondi Lunguzi Njawala

As I leave here I am very optimist about what lies ahead.
As I leave here I will go with a smile
for I know you are also smiling.
As I leave here I carry with me joys of sisterhood.

As I leave here I know the heavens are rejoicing.
For when I prayed, they promised me joy.
Truly, my prayers were answered.
For I myself I feel satisfied.
As I leave here I carry beauty
of the uniqueness of each and every one of you.

As I leave here I know we are going to embrace change.
For I know we have been exposed to great earnings.
New disciplines.
New understandings.
Above all, to love and appreciate each other just as we are.

Change the way you look at things
and the things you look at change.

I Hold a Key

Chikondi Lunguzi Njawala

I hold a key
Look at the key that I picked
I picked a rusty key because
all the good keys were already taken
Hmm! Sometimes life is like a rusty key
to many girls,
Nobody wants you
No-one admires you
People despise you for nothing
People ignore you for no reason.

You feel depressed
You feel oppressed
You are weak to respond
You are weak to stand up for yourself
No voice to speak up and speak out
Struggling to find yourself
Or song of hope.

Can I rise up to greatness?
Yes, you can
A sound of a still voice
Ringing in your ears
Troubled by challenges faced
And the unknown fear of what may rise ahead.

As you slowly build your confidence
Never look back

Ignore the voice that says no you can't,
she is better than you.
Keep standing on your toes till when you find your feet
Try to be in control till when you are fully fit
Be a girl with a true voice and walk the talk.

Dip your rusty key in hope
and create within yourself a life of peace
Keep trying to open till when it actually opens.

For All The Girls Coming After Me

Chikondi Lunguzi Njawala

Always drive to be the best of yourself
The best of your abilities
Walk with your heads high
regardless how dark the clouds get
Work hard in school
To others, this chance never come
Remember life is a journey
With potholes along the way.

Live life to the fullest
Obey the elders
For they are wiser
They have seen many days
Live your life not that of others.

Be satisfied with the present
Stay focused
Live to love not to hate
Always know when to walk away
and do it with dignity
Choose the career you love
so it never feels like you are working.

Think big,
Stay positive and
And leave gap for disappointments.
Always remember to stand still
in disappointments,
waves never last forever.

Keep your souls young
and live life to the fullest.

Keep writing, keep reading
Continue to believe in your dreams.
Love you all!

My future will be different because…..

Chikondi Lunguzi Njawala

I know I have my father by my side,
he lives in heaven and yet he lives in me.
I have Jesus as my Lord and saviour.
I have the Holy Spirit who acts on my behalf.
He who carries the solution to all my problems.
Those fears and
His gentle nature reminds me
to work on my weaknesses.
I know I am safe in this dwelling place.
I know my future will be different.

My future will be different
My days will be brighter
When I look back I will smile
Knowing that I have made a difference
Difference in one's life

My future will be different because
I have learnt to look at things differently
I know that I am unique
I know that I have a voice

Chikondi Lunguzi Njawala is a goal-oriented woman who believes that with leadership, guidance and resources we can create a brighter future for the girl child. She has an MSc in Marketing and a Post Graduate Diploma from the Chartered Institute of Marketing (CIM). She is passionate about working with young girls and women.

Chikondi served as Program Manager for VoiceFlame's writing programs in Malawi from 2015 – 2018. A job highlight for her was to travel to the US where she was able to experience and embrace a reading and writing culture and tailor-make a similar programme for school girls in Malawi.

She understands the importance of education for females and dedicates herself to lead and strengthen girls to stay in school. She encourages girls to embrace reading and writing as a means to self and community empowerment. In 2014, Chikondi was trained as an Amherst Writers & Artists writing facilitator.

Improve? Yes, There is Room

Cynthia Mtseka

Cynthia Mtseka lives in Lilongwe, Malawi. She is a journalist focusing on female empowerment and early childhood development. Many people in Malawi are fighting for the rights of girls, women and children but this does not mean we cannot hold hands and fight alongside them. There is more we can do, and we must fight for the rights of these vulnerable groups until violence against them is eliminated.

I am Cynthia Mtseka. I was born in 1996 in Lilongwe, Malawi and I am currently a board member at VoiceFlame Malawi.

I was born to very humble beginnings and I never thought I would reach this far. It sometimes seems like a joke when I remember the days when I was a five year old in standard one at Son Shine Private School at Kawale Township in Lilongwe.

My primary school days were good in that if my teacher was told to pick the ten brightest students in the class, I would surely be included. There were bad days because I attended a private school and would see my friends having better things than I did. Additionally, most of my classmates were very selective and would choose whom to associate with based on where that person was from and the things they brought to school.

When I was 9 years old I changed schools and I moved to Holy Family Private School at Chilinde Township in the same city of Lilongwe. The two years that I spent at the school were really a blessing to me. I was mostly in position 2 and a few times position 1 which highly motivated me. Every time I reached a position higher than two I would work harder to get an even better position. I felt accepted, as most of the people at the school were within my class.

When I was 12, I started my final primary school class, Standard 8. I went to a government primary school called Kamuzu Barracks Primary School.

It was challenging at times being in a class of more than 100 students, and the teachers there were a bit harsh compared to the teachers at the private school. My grades were not bad at this school.

I was very bad at mathematics since standard one but I told myself that it is not a bad thing because I did far better in other subjects. This was a very bad decision because it affected me greatly in all of my other studies. I was so poor at mathematics that it affected my scores in sciences, because science also involves mathematics.

I want to encourage everyone who thinks that not doing well in any one subject is okay. Never overlook a weak point, because by doing so you will never improve and there will come a moment when you will regret your decision. You can improve today, not tomorrow, as today is the only chance you have to improve. Tomorrow is a mystery and may never come. Each tomorrow will bring its own challenges for you to defeat.

Secondary School

I finished my primary school, and by the grace of God I was selected to attend Likuni Girls Secondary School in the city of Lilongwe, one of the National secondary schools in Malawi. Likuni is a boarding school and I was so happy to be selected to enroll there. I thought things would be as easy as they were in primary school, but I lied to myself, here was where I learnt life is not easy. If I were told to rewind my life, I would choose to skip my secondary school days.

I was still not a fan of mathematics and did not want to improve but I now needed to take the subject of Physical Science, consisting of physics and chemistry. Likuni was a national secondary school comprised of the best girl students in the country. In primary school I would be in the top 10 in my class but in secondary school I was not even in the best 70. No matter how hard I worked, it became harder for me. I was bad at Mathematics and worse at Physical Science. I was learning Physical Science because it was compulsory but hated it more than I hated hunger.

A problem that contributed to my failure in mathematics was that I disliked my math teacher of form 1 and 2. My math teacher happened to be my form 1 teacher. She knew me very well as one of the students who failed mathematics. The fact that she knew this made me hate her even more because when she taught math she would ask the class if we understood. The whole class, including me would say "Yes," but then she would say (in her Zimbabwean accent) "Cynthia, even you too are saying you have understood?" I would think to myself "Why does this Zimbabwean hate me this much?" But, the truth is that she really was right. I never understood anything.

In 2010 I wrote my Junior Certificate Examinations (JCE). My overall grade was B (very good) with a C (good) in mathematics and a D (average) in physical science. This D came because of my shallow knowledge of mathematics, which is at the core of many professions. If you want to be an engineer and you fail mathematics you must realize that you are cheating yourself and you have to pull up your socks.

Science is like a car, and for that car to move it needs an engine, and in this case mathematics is the engine of science. If you want to be a doctor, but your grades are as small a child's shoe then you are chasing after the wind. If girls do not like mathematics and sciences and get bad grades in these subjects, they will have limited chances to go to the university, as most universities in Malawi want students who have good grades in their Malawi School Certificate of Education. It is not impossible for a person without sciences to go to the university but the chances are slim because most public universities want students with good grades in sciences. It is far better to qualify in all programs at university rather than allowing your grades to limit you. You may end up choosing professions you do not want because you have no choice.

I got to senior secondary school classes form 3 and 4 where things got worse each passing day. Our school report cards were sent to our parents while we were already at school for the next term. I remember that my mother photocopied a report card and sent me the copy with a note saying "Asisi koma kukhoza kumeneku kutipindulira," (my sister, will these kinds of grades profit us?). I felt pity for myself.

I wrote my Malawi School Certificate of Education and passed with a weak credit in mathematics and a pass in physical science. This really affected me as I wanted to be a medical doctor, but with my grades this was not possible. The other profession I wanted to study was Civil Engineering but could not for the same reason nor could I study agriculture because it too required a credit in physical science. I applied to the country's public university but was not selected.

I applied for a Diploma in Journalism at the University of Malawi where I was enrolled, but the going got even tougher there. I was used to my secondary school habits of memorizing things but realized that College examinations require one to apply knowledge. I corrected my weak points and finished my diploma with a pass. I now know that if I had corrected my weak points earlier I could have gotten a credit. I am however, thankful to God for what I got and through it all I learnt a lot. Finding and correcting my mistakes was the best experience ever and had I taken time to realize and correct my mistakes in secondary school I could have been in the profession that I wanted. There is no time for regrets and in my current profession I can still become my best.

In the Media Industry

It took six months to find a job. I started an internship at one of the country's smallest radio stations which gave me the opportunity to meet the program manager of VoiceFlame. Currently I am one of the board members of VoiceFlame Malawi and even though the future seemed dark at the beginning I can now gladly say the future is promising and I am happy. The best days are in my future.

I realize now that during my secondary school days I did not lack motivation, I simply lacked the courage to improve. People often say that if you want to be a winner, walk around with winners and you too will win. I was and still am best friends with one of the best performing girls in our class, but I did not become one of the best. It's clear that just roaming with the best people is not a guarantee that you will become the best in life, you must choose to be the best. You must work hard to become the best version of you, and if nothing seems to go your way, don't worry. Just keep on working at it, success is not for quitters.

Another secret of a successful life is to continue to learn, wherever you may be. We are not where we are by accident. Every experience and every place where we find ourselves is a place to learn. It does not matter that you may not like where you are or what you do. Today's experience will help you somewhere or somehow. Life is unpredictable and often not a bed of roses because where there are roses there are also thorns. In a bee hive you find honey as well as bees and one must choose to either be a coward and runaway or risk getting the stings and the honey. Always remember that life is never free of challenges. We must defeat the challenge of today and meet the challenge tomorrow and defeat it. There is always room for improvement.

From a Rural Nobody to an Urban Somebody

Demetria Banda

Demetria Herman Banda was born on 29 June 1995. She is a Malawian by nationality and single. She is the second born in a family of five, the sister of two girls and two boys. She was born and grew up in various households due to a poor divorced family. Both her father and mother were not educated and not employed. Demetria comes from Mbingwa Village T/A Mduwa in Mchinji District. She was only told that her mother and father divorced for unknown reasons when Demetria was only two years old in 1997.

She has surpassed various stresses to access school fees as well as devote time to concentrate on education. She trusts that her past experience has nothing to do with her success and her ongoing persistence in continuing with her university education is the recipe for her success. Each challenge she encounters requires her to think analytically and logically to achieve her dream, the desire for university education and any further education thereafter.

I envy and admire people who have been brought up in an environment of plenty, getting what they want at the press of a button. But there are others, people like me that don't get things on a silver platter, who must toil day in and day out as they create their chosen pathways to rise and shine. I am a living example of a young person who dares to surmount frustration and carry on amidst discomfort as I climb mountains of hope en route to satisfy my craving for education.

I was born and grew up in a poor family since both my father and mother were not educated and not employed. I knew that my mother and father divorced for unknown reasons while I was only two years old, in 1997. In 1998 I went to stay with my father and my step mother. Life with my step mother was not exciting, but was full of miseries. At only three years old I expected to be at my mum's lap but missed this sense of belonging to a mother. My step mother did not give me enough support or attention, yet I keenly observed how she favoured her biological daughter. I started standard one in 1999 when I was only four years old. I repeated standard two then went to stay with my uncle who was teaching at Mponda Primary School in Mchinji district. I was thinking that the best way to work hard in my education is to stay closer to my uncle because he was trying hard to encourage me in terms of my education. I was only six years old when I went to stay with my uncle.

My uncle migrated to Ludzi Trading Center when I was in standard five and he would cycle daily from Ludzi to Mponda village. During this time I went back to Mbingwa Village to stay with my dad while I had reached standard 3 in 2001. I started reading Chichewa books when I was in standard two and was reading at a standard 6 level. As a result I was loved by more teachers at school.

I learned at Mbingwa primary school until standard five when my uncle got married and adopted me to be his first daughter, as he was starting a new family. In 2006 when I was in standard 6, I went to live with my uncle and aunt in Dowa District and learnt at Dowa 1 Primary School. My performance was fair and as such my uncle began both supporting me and encouraging me, an easy thing for him to do because he was a primary school teacher.

I wrote standard 8 exams in 2009 but did not do well so my uncle advised that I repeat the class. My uncle justified that I may have not done well because he had gone to Malawi College of Health Sciences in 2007 while my aunt went to Nkhoma College of Nursing and Midwifery. The couple had left their first born daughter who was only 6 months old under the care of my uncle's sister, Maureen and me. To an extent that I agreed this was indeed a hindrance as we had little time to concentrate on school work. I had little time for studies because after my classes I had to take care of the child while Maureen was learning at Robert Blake Secondary School.

In 2010 my uncle and aunt completed their studies and sent me to Ludzi Girls Boarding Primary School. I faced another challenge for I could not meet the demands of a new syllabus. I worked extra hard and I tried my luck at writing Catholic mission exams. Luckily, I was offered a place at

Ludzi Community Day Secondary School but had to request a transfer to Kochilira Community Day Secondary School because Ludzi Secondary School was very far from my father's residence.

I still had to cover close to 10 kilometers from home to Kochilira Community Day Secondary school I surmounted the situation because it was better than the Ludzi scenario. It was nearly impossible to study because I always returned from school so late in the afternoon that there was no time for me to open my books to study even during the evening.

Surprisingly, when results for Catholic exams were released I had been selected to Likuni Girl's Secondary School. I was very happy because this was a school where I had longed to do my learning. My dream school had come into reality. But this happiness was short lived for soon I realized life was getting tougher than I anticipated in terms of financial support. It turned out that within a short time of getting financial support both from father and uncle, my uncle got another chance to continue with his studies. The two had worked together to pay my fees.

My father was always there for me and they both helped each other to pay my school fees including providing me with upkeep money, but the tribulations heightened when I was in form three. My uncle started school again and he was paying school fees for himself, and it became difficult for him to continue paying for me.

My father tried to pay the fees, but it was very hard since my dad is unemployed and his main source of financial income was through farming. As a subsistence farmer his farm efforts would not earn him enough for a family, let alone for my fees. I admit that I appreciated my uncle's efforts but noticed that his energy was dropping. He was also aging and no longer had the energy to reach my financial expectations.

At one point my father went to request at Mchinji social welfare for financial support which eventually materialized. This became another hassle because the social welfare office was not efficient in its student support which led to our school administration chasing us away. We lagged behind in terms of lessons since our classmates continued learning. Though I later managed to return it was hard to catch up.

The trend recurred when I was in my third semester of form four when I was chased from school and stayed home for more than three weeks, only returning to school to write mock exams. When results of the Malawi School Certificate of Exam came out I was not surprised that I had failed, with 41 points. I did not like my failure situation and decided to rewrite. This time I managed to pass.

I defied my situation of lack such that I obtained 18 points at MSCE in 2014. This was one exciting time during which I defied the odds. I was staying at Kaware with my mother's sister Maureen and wanted to sit for university entrance exams but my mother's sister could not support me to pay for coaching fees. Then there came a time when the university entry system changed. We were no longer expected to write university entry exams, but were advised to just fill the forms of National Council for Higher Education (NCHE). I hesitated for some time but later developed the courage to once again bother my father to finance my university education.

I was lucky that he sent me K5,000 while my uncle sent me K3,000, a total of eight thousand kwacha which was enough to be deposited because the form was K7,000. However, when I analyzed the other expenses which I required, I noted the money was insufficient to complete the process of sending the forms. I tried to seek support from my mother's sister I was staying with in Kawale but she told me she did not have any money to spare for my sake. I knelt down and prayed for an open gate of financial support. I trusted that someday I was going to make it, because God is never late.

To go from one point to another I had to walk the dusty roads of Lilongwe as I arrived from Kawale to Lilongwe town and then back. Life was getting tougher because I also had to walk from Kawale to HB house at Chilambula road just to collect forms. Because I had not yet developed literary competence I kept making mistakes such that I had to fill out the form several times.

When the final date of submission was due I thought it wise to sell my chitenje, or fabric wrap which was given to me as a remembrance while at secondary school and eventually managed to deposit the needed finances for my application form. I recall that on the day I went to HB house to deliver my form I realized I had remained with only k50 in my pocket. This would not suffice to purchase an envelope into which I was to seal the form. I sat on a tree trunk wondering and imagining an envelope flying past me so that I could grasp it. Then, I looked up to heaven and clasped my hands. I saw a friend of mine approaching and when I told her my situation she gave me k100, which was enough to submit the form. My face was beaming as I slipped the form into the envelope and submitted it.

In 2015 I was selected to the Malawi Polytechnic. My happiness was short lived as this turned out to be the next thorn in my flesh and I spent many nights crying for God's wonders. During the day I pretended to be normal to conceal my deep rooted financial problems. I could not afford to pay my tuition fees, upkeep allowance and accommodation fee. Then, a distant relation whom I called a sister, invited me to stay with her at Chitawira location. Later I applied for a student loan but like other needy students my request fell on a blank wall. The consequence of this was that I couldn't access my examination number.

A friend of mine encouraged me to inform the dean of students who helped me to access the exam number despite not having paid. I thanked my Lord for the wonder as I sat for exams. Back at home my so called sister started mistreating me. She suspected that since I often reported back home late, that I must have a boyfriend and further accused me of being rude and stubborn. My performance begun to decline once more.

Life turned fairer on me in 2016 when I eventually secured a loan and was given a place at the campus hostel. Again luck struck me as I was sponsored by Tertiary Education Scholarship Trust (TEST). I still lament that accommodation and upkeep finances remain a challenge since am a self sponsored student. Indeed I still find it tough to meet my needs and requirements, but I praise myself for being a search warrior to ensure that I don't drop out.

As I am talking I am now in my third academic year studying for a Bachelor of Arts in journalism at The University of Malawi The Polytechnic. I sincerely hope that I will graduate and become someone. I agree that problems I endure invite critical thinking as to what step to take. Remember, my strides are important since I am the only girl in my village who has made it to university and the only one in my family that has gone this far with education.

This is just a partial account of the thorns that keep pricking my hands and body as I continuously search for my gold medal education. I really feel privileged that despite the hassles I was among the short listed students to study at the University of Malawi the Polytechnic, and I am sure this will be part of history someday.

I Had a Dream

Elizabeth Kajasiche

Elizabeth was born on 4th December, 1964. She is the ninth born in a family of twelve, ten girls and two boys. She comes from Chilota Village, Traditional Authority Njewa in Lilongwe District Malawi. She did her primary education at Chigoneka primary school and was selected to Lilongwe Girls secondary school in 1981 and finished in 1985 June.

Elizabeth went to Lilongwe teachers training college from 1985 to 1987. After graduation, she taught for nine years then was appointed deputy headteacher for Bunda primary school in 1996. In 2006 she went to African Bible College to pursue a bachelor's degree in Christian Education and obtained her B.A in 2010. She has been a secondary school teacher ever since.

I was born in a family of ten girls and two boys and grew up in a Christian family. My parents were devoted Presbyterians. Our village was situated in the suburbs of Lilongwe city. It is located in between Area 47 and The Army Air wing. During my school going time schools were far apart. It was not easy for one to go to school as it was a distance of about eight kilometres to and eight from. Coming from a poor family I was going to school bare footed and was eating no breakfast and with no packed meal.

All this time I had a dream to become a teacher. One day as I was on my way to school I sat down, looked at beautiful houses with electricity and running water in Area 47 and asked myself what was the key to occupy these houses? The answer was education. From that day I started working very hard that I didn't want anybody to beat me in class. My ambition was to be among the top ten. Things went in very well that I managed to pass my primary school leaving certificate examination and was selected to Lilongwe Girls Secondary school.

While at school life was not simple. Sometimes I could go to school late because of lack of school fees. Sometimes I could go to school without pocket money, but my intention was to get a paper. I worked hard and managed to get the Malawi School Certificate. I didn't make it to the university in the first place. So I did my tertiary education at the teacher's training college and qualified as a primary school teacher. I told my mom that I am not a primary school teacher.

After serving for four years I was appointed to a deputy headteacher. It was not easy for me to do such a work. But with time I got used to it and loved my work so much. In 2001 I was invited to participate in curriculum reformation. It was a good platform where I gained more exposure and from there I got a courage to apply for an upgrading. This was the time my dreams came true. The dream to become the secondary school teacher. I went to African Bible College to pursue my bachelor's degree.

Life has not been simple from the time I graduated from the college. My husband stopped working and my two children were now going to college. Being a woman I did not look down at myself. I stood up to care for my children. I managed to educate them. Now they are all graduates.

How I Struggled With My Education

Fiddy Lundu

Fiddy Mtema is the eighth born daughter in a family of twelve children born to the late Naphtal and Rosalia Mtema. She hails from Mchinji District, Tembwe village Traditional Authority Mlonyeni, and is married to Aubrey Lundu.

She has a bachelor's degree in arts majoring in English, obtained in 2017 at The Catholic University of Malawi, a diploma in education obtained at Domasi College of Education in 2011, a Diploma in Special Needs Education obtained in 2017 at Montfort college and a certificate in Special Needs Education obtained in 2006 at the same college. She is also in possession of a T2 teaching Certificate obtained in 1992 at St Joseph Teachers Training College in Dedza District.

Currently Fiddy is Head of Department in Special Needs Education at Lunzu Secondary School. However, life has not been easy for her to complete all of her studies. She has a family and people to take care of, who suffered socially, physically, spiritually and financially during this training. As a mother, she was supposed to encourage her children to go to school, church and to buy clothes and food, which was not possible during that time. She used all of her salary for school fees, food, photocopies, transport and accommodation. There were times that she had to borrow money from school to use for transport and on occasion had to sleep on an empty stomach because she had no money.

To crown it all, she thanks her husband, colleagues and lecturers for their service and words of encouragement to make her who she is today. She went from a primary school teacher to a secondary school teacher and to God be the glory. Her ambition is to proceed with a master's degree, the only challenge will again be the money for fees.

My name is Fiddy Mtema Lundu, the 8th born daughter of the late Naphtal and Rosaria Mtema. I was born in a family of six boys and six girls. My father was working under Ministry of Labour as a District Labour

Officer while my mother was a housewife. Despite our family being large, my parents had the welfare of the family at heart and they did all they could to help us get our education.

I started my education from a nursery school when I was only two years old. When I was six years old I went to St. Pius where I started standard one in 1978. I can say I was brilliant during those years because I never repeated a class, until I reached standard eight. As I was about to write my Primary School Leaving Certificate in 1984, I developed heartache but did not give up and in all these years I got a pass.

My father sent me to Ludzi Girls Boarding Primary School in 1985. Some of my friends did not like the trend of repeating this class so they made their way to Malawi Correspondence College which I did not want to attend. I decided to repeat Standard 8 until I was selected to Lilongwe Girls Secondary School in 1986.

Life was not all that easy because it was my first time to stay far away from my parents. Because of the migraine headache problem that I was experiencing, my parents had wanted me close to them so they could easily monitor my health. Their concerns had to be set aside because there was no other option. My education was more important than anything else so eventully I got used to it.

In class I faced a lot of challenges during mathematics. I hated this subject and no matter how much effort the teacher put in, I never succeeded. In 1990, I wrote the Malawi School Certificate Examinations which I passed, but the grades were not good enough to go to any university. Early on I had thought I would be eligible for selection to the Bunda College of Agriculture but did not qualify. The only option was to apply for teaching and I was successful such that I underwent a two year training with a T2 teaching Certificate at St Joseph Teachers Training College. I came out of college in 1992 and joined the teaching profession that same year.

After teaching for thirteen years, I composed myself and stood firm to go back into school. I started attending classes at Mthunzi Private Secondary School in 2005. It was not easy because I had to go to work in the morning and in the afternoon had to attend to lessons. By then the curriculum had changed completely but I still did not give up. I had to fight tooth to nail to get what I wanted and eventually managed to get good grades, including mathematics.

In 2006, I saw a vacancy in the newspaper for Special Needs Education at Montfort College. I applied for the position and was successful. The course was to run for one full year. At this juncture, I could see the fruits of reducing the grades and upon completion of the course was awarded a certificate as a specialist teacher. I was then posted to Kamuzu Primary School where I had a resource centre where I started teaching students with special needs. I really enjoyed teaching these learners because to me it was an eye opener. I never thought such learners could receive an education but that was not true. Disability is not inability.

I never tired of upgrading myself, so while at Montfort College I applied for a diploma course at Domasi College. I was called for the interviews but did not succeed. I never gave up, applied for the course in 2007 but again was not successful. I did the same in 2008, was successful and commenced the three year course in January, 2009. Upon graduation in February 2012 I was posted to Lunzu Secondary School as a specialist teacher to teach students with special needs. In 2013, I was among the specialist teachers who were chosen to pursue a diploma course in Special Needs Education at Montfort College for three years. The course was to be done on holidays while the school children were on holiday.

I did not tire of furthering my education so in 2014 I applied for a degree course at The Catholic University of Malawi. I was accepted and was expected to resume the course starting with intensive learning in December, 2014 which I did. However this was a challenge in terms of time management because I then had two courses at hand which were to be run concurrently while including work and taking care of my family.

On one hand, I was happy because the diploma and degree courses were all done at Montfort College, Nguludi campus and the diploma course was sponsored by the Government of Malawi. I only had to pay tuition, on the other hand I had to pay for the degree course.

I nearly had to drop the degree course when I was in my final year when my husband was admitted to Mlambe Hospital which meant that I had to stop attending to my university study in order to care for him. Luckily enough the break was not too long and as soon as he got a bit better we were discharged.

I completed the diploma course in December 2015 including teaching practice while the degree course was completed in December 2016. The battle was still not over because I was left with my dissertation which was to be defended in June 2017. All went well, and I graduated on 30th September 2017 with a Bachelor of Arts degree in Education and on 18th December 2017 with a Diploma in Special Needs Education with a specialty on students with learning difficulties.

I believe that my hard work and endurance has taken me this far. God has really done wonders in my life, otherwise I could not have been where I am now. Imagine going from a primary school teacher with a T2 teaching certificate to a secondary school teacher with a degree. I thank my parents, relatives, husband and children and say to God be the glory.

My Destination

Gladys James

Gladys James is 18 years old, She is the sixth born in a family of seven children. Born on 4 January 2000. Her parents are from Balaka and Machinga, my home village. She stays in Lilongwe district together with her parents and did her primary school at Poly and Kamkodola School up to standard eight. She was selected for Chigoneka day secondary school up to form 4 where she sat for Malawi Living Secondary Certificate Education and was able to get 22 points. Her passion is to become a nurse. She applied to universities that offer nursing programs and two of the universities, Mulanje and Deayang Universities offered her a place to study nursing. Because she was already selected and studying animal heath at Lilongwe University of Agriculture and Natural resources, NRC CAMPUS in a diploma course, her dream is to upgrade to a nursing program.

They say women are weak and fearful. But I say we are strong enough to stand and speak out our thoughts, we are just lacking the empowerment across the world wide. Here is a young and passionate women with a dream, hoping that one day women's and girls' life will change for good. A young woman feels uncomfortable when girls are always the victims in every situation.

My name is Gladys, I was born in the family of Mr. and Mrs. James. I was approximately six years old when my parents sent me to school at Poly private school then I continued to Kamkodola primary where I sat for my junior certificate of education.

In standard 8 I discovered my dream when Mrs Daniel visited my school. She was a nurse by profession, her words inspired me a lot and I made a decision to become a nurse like her. I was curious to hear more about her story. She had a story that inspired me, and I believe that the story she was holding can inspire thousands of women and girls who need encouragement like I did. Honestly her words moistures my thirst inside my throat, I was like ''Please Mrs don't stop telling us the story."

Since then I developed a habit of reading and I listened to the news on the radio in my free time. In 2013 I sat for my junior certificate of education and I was able to pass with flying colours. Unexpectedly, I wasn't selected to any secondary school so instead I started going to an open school to progress in my studies.

Life completely changed in secondary school. I was happy to find a friend, Mphatso, who kept me company. I discovered that we have the same goal to go far with our education. Our difference was that she wanted to become a social worker, while I wanted to become a nurse. I was happy to find such a caring, kind friend that I was missing all that time.

Adding to my dream, I was also passionate about writing and my dream is to become a writer. My stories and poems always guarantee women and girls empowerment. In my writings I believe that women are unique and powerful. One of my famous poems was Albinism, which I wrote aiming to stop eliminating the violence toward our fellow friends, the albinos. I wrote it after listening to the news on the radio, that one woman with albino skin had been killed at her own garden.

I was furious and expressed my anger in the paper. The following day I sang my poem at the assembly time at school. "Yes it is our responsibility to change the mind set of people." That was one of my sentences that I wrote in my poem. My fellow students were shocked with the poem, some even called me albino just because of that poem, and that day I felt that writing was indeed powerful and has the ability to meet people in an easier way.

It was in term two, when I was selected to start a day secondary school at Chigoneka. This was like healing the wounds in my vein. I had to wake up early in the morning to do some chores before going to school. I studied hard and competed with my fellow student and was always in the top ten.

One day, one of the young women Chikondi Lunguzi, visited our school and introduced me to writers club. I couldn't wait to register my name in the club. Chikondi was a kind and loving woman who encouraged us to speak our imagination. She opened our minds with her inspiring story. In her I found the full encouragement I wanted.

Life was good at secondary level but another side of life seemed bitter. Sometimes I thought I wouldn't be able to pursue my education because of the challenges I met. Unexpectedly my lovely father got sick. He wasn't able to work. Tears of fear and hopelessness flowed on my face.

I was afraid of failing to achieve my goals since my father was the only person paying for my school fees and was the only one who encouraged me a lot, mostly when he began telling me his past story.

My father is such a kind person who liked talking a lot. He is the only child in his family, he had no brother and sisters whom I can call uncle and aunt respectively. His story carries sorrow starting from his birth and family life. His mother hadn't been able to bear a child for five years. My father was the only blessing in his family. But during his birth my father seemed like he was about to die, having difficulties in his breathing, all the people thought the child had no more life to that extent people decided to dig his grave, but suddenly, by the grace of God he arose in his normal breathing, that was the beginning of his life.

As the only child in his family my father had to encounter the big responsibility to look after his parents. You could think how village life is. A poor child found it difficult to go far with his education instead he travelled to town to look for a job. While in town he found that life was more bitter than he expected. He had to walk miles barefooted in searching for a job and gladly enough my father was secured a job as a plumber at the State House.

My father usually spoke to me that, though he did not go far with his education, the children must be educated. But at this sickness time I missed all the words he usually said. What was remaining inside me was only memories, sometimes I could feel that my father's dream would never be fulfilled. I couldn't pay attention in class, and all of this happened when I was in form 3. Unbelievably VoiceFlame brought back my hope and paid my fees. The sudden fresh air enters my throat. I hadn't expected that golden chance in my life ''God is good for everyone" was my song'.

My father began to get better and hearing the good news, it was like healing the pains in his sickness. Life was changed. Now my English teacher becomes a friend of mine, a teacher who knows his job of teaching. The encouragement I got from him was like adding more salt to a pain wound. ''My dearest student work hard and you will make it," Mr Banda always spoke to me, and his voice of encouragement brought that courage inside me.

In 2017 was my time to sit for my Malawi secondary certificate education. Here I have to yield more time to read. I had to wake up early in the morning to go to school so that I could read, since my school had no library and laboratory. I had to be outside to read. Looking at the condition of my school, I come up with another poem, which I sang during my graduation ceremony, the poem was aiming to have school materials. At this ceremony I was awarded in Biology, agriculture and life skills for being a best student in those subjects. I could hear my quick intake of breath every seconds. I hadn't expected that in my life.

It was 25 days remaining for me to write the examination. I was afraid as some were in mathematics subject, therefore I decided to add some practice times in mathematics but this had to be done after classes at 4 p.m. At this time in our religion we fast, therefore after classes I had to walk some miles to Mtsiliza while fasting, where I had maths part times there and we were ending between 9 p.m. to 10 p.m.

My father complained for my working at night and for being a young girl and tried to stopped me since he felt I was putting my life in danger. But I didn't agree with his idea to stopped me, instead I comfort him and made him understand me. I said to my father, "If I will stay just because I am a girl, I will remain staying at the same level and never go far with education." I begged him to be strong for me. My father had no choice than to allow me. Here was when I realised the power of using my voice.

I continued to go to Mtsiliza up until I wrote my Malawi secondary certificate of education. After wrote my examination Chikondi Lunguzi our matron of writer's club introduced to me and my friend a menstrual pad project which was sponsored by the founder of VoiceFlame Mary Tuchscherer from America. The aim of the project was to keep girls in school. VoiceFlame had found that some of the girls are not able to go to school because of menstrual period. Therefore had to come up with the project to distribute free pads in a lot of schools, and we did after our sewing pads. At the end of the months VoiceFlame paid us.

After the examination was realised, I got 22 points. Yes they were good points, but this didn't satisfied me but only bring more tears to my eyes. I hadn't expected such kind of points, but lucky enough I had a good grade in science subject and was able to be selected at Lilongwe University of Agriculture and Natural Resources, NRC Campus studying for a diploma in animal health. I was also chosen by Mulanje and Deayang University to study nursing. But I couldn't go to those university since I was already schooling at NRC campus. Here at NRC, VoiceFlame is paying for my fees. And since my aim was to become a nurse, Gladys is hoping that after the diploma she has to go far and upgrade as a nurse.

Myself I believe that with our mind and heart together with our strength we can change Malawi. But it starts with developing ourselves before changing Malawi. Since we can't talk about Malawi without talking about the people living in it, remember there can't be a country without people, meaning us as people. We are the ones who make up Malawi.

Women, wake up and stop looking down on ourselves and be ready to voice out our thoughts and imaginations. Together we will smile happy tears. Girls, believe indeed that we are the future leaders. Please to some of the organisations. We need you to come out from where you been hidden and join the work VoiceFlame has started and reach as many girls. We actually need your help.

Achievement of My Desired Vision

Juliana Banda

I am a young lady aged 17, am a Malawian born in a family of six and I am the fifth. I started my primary school when I was five years old at Chigoneka Primary School where I was selected to Mkwichi Secondary School.

I started my secondary school at thirteen and my secondary life has been so good though there were many challenges along the road. But I used to control myself from things that could put my life in danger until I wrote my final secondary examination. After the results of my final secondary exams fortunately I was selected to Chancellor College and now am waiting for the exact time of starting my program there.

A woman is a person who can do anything just as a man though obstacles are everywhere. But there's always a great achievement if she never look down on herself, this is my journey to success.

When I was a little girl I had a passion of being someone like a role model to a lot of people. But my problem was that I used to follow other people's dreams. I remember when I was very young I used to say I want to be a lawyer just because my brother told me he wanted to be a lawyer. But whenever I see a nurse I found myself considering the nursing profession and if I see a journalist I get the innate desire of taking up that profession. It was a complicated career choice that even in class when our teacher in class ask who we wanted to be, I would say a lawyer. After hearing other people's career choices I would prefer to follow their choices than mine. I didn't really know what I want in life.

One day after opening a newspaper I saw there was a woman and there was also her true life story and the most attractive thing that made me to read the story was her name. Her name was Juliana and that's my name too. Inside the woman's story there were words that inspired me. Some of the words were sticking to me. Know what you believe and never give up on you're dream. These words made me realize that I believe in becoming a lawyer, but I don't follow this dream and I always give up on this dream whenever I hear other people's dreams. From that day I decided to be a lawyer and I got a passion of studying law at one of the public universities. This woman I saw

in the newspaper really helped my education, help me to follow my dreams and achieve my goals.

Following my dreams was quite interesting though there were many setbacks because there is no smooth road to success. One of the challenges I faced was the environment I was living in. I stay in such a noisy place because there a lot of bars and every night its noisy, so I was failing to study because of the noise. This was really an obstacle to my education.

Another setback was lacking encouragement from my relatives because though I used to tell them that I wanted to go to university to study law, many of them were discouraging me by giving negative comments on my dream just because no one in my family has ever gone to one of the public universities of Malawi. I was giving up but I looked around, I hear the voice of how I'm going to fulfill my dreams and the words never give up your dream always come in my mind. Due to this challenge my performance was declining. Then my dad asked me why my performance changed. I told him that it was because my studies were discouraged by the noise we experience at night from the bars.

My dad told me that he is going to send me to one of our relatives, but I didn't accept the idea of sending me to our relative because it was very far from my school and I couldn't manage to walk a long distance. Then I choose to find help from my neighbour Steve. He told me that I should be doing my studies at school in the library. This advice helped me a lot because my performance little by little was rising again.

RISING TO THE CHALLENGE

Linley Mayenda

Linley Mayenda was born in 1996 in the outskirts of Blantyre and is a poet and spoken word performer. Her performance on stage is eye catching and thrilling to watch. She is currently a student at Eastern Collage of Law and holds a diploma in legal studies and is a member of Reflections of Art and PEN Malawi. She is currently assembling her poetry pieces so that one day her poetry book, "Voices" can be published.

Wise people say that when one educates just one girl then it is like educating the whole community and a nation at large. Nelson Mandela, the late president of South Africa who fought against apartheid for decades, kept reminding fellow Africans that education is the key to success. Indeed, everyone would like to use this important key to open the door out of poverty and into success. However, as an African girl it seems the saying may not materialize unless the girl works extra hard compared to boys.

Being a girl has made it difficult to attain my education. I am not the only one who has undergone challenges in attaining an education, but the difference is that I have not fallen down to challenges. I grew up in a culture where male dominance is the order and even our history has passed from generation to generation advising girls that they are under male authority and are men's property. As such, women have grown up feeling the socially constructed inferiority norms, attitudes and behaviours and conform to society's expected behaviours for women. The courageous women, who stood their ground to conquer this belief were laughed at, or their marriages broke up. Men would say, "This woman also puts on a trouser, so she wants to be a man just as I am," or called nasty names like "bitches." These names are used, just because they tried to oppose men as they struggled to gain recognition in society.

Despite being brought up in this environment I taught myself that I can become whatever I want even though I am female. Our family expected me to do household chores before I went to school and again after returning home. I did not have as much time to study as the boys because there was a distance to go and fetch water and my head would be very heavy by the time I returned with a bucket of water. I would bathe in cold water and set off for school in the morning, often times on an empty stomach because there was no food in our home. I was often late for school because of the work I did before getting water to bathe and leave for school. Once I arrived at school late I was punished. Over the years I have taught myself that I must manage my time if am to go far with my education. Despite these circumstances I have fought with persistence and determination, full of enthusiasm, holding my head high knowing that am more than what society sees in me.

Things came to almost a standstill when I was selected to go to university. My father knew that education was important for me, even though I am a girl child. He did his best by running various businesses and my mother helped my father to make ends meets so that I could get a university degree. All along I have learnt that passing or failing in school is a result of one's choice, and no one is born dull just because she is a female. It is the choice of each person to make others proud.

Now, I live to prove that it is wrong to discourage a girl from attaining education. I now live a life that is not determined by what others have said or may think. I currently have my diploma in law but am not yet where I would like to be. I will continue my education, time and circumstances permitting. I am a warrior who continues to strive for greatness no matter what hindrances I have gone through, or the thorns and pricks that come on my route to education.

There were those who used to mock my mother for marrying a poor man and that she would continue to face financial hardships. I know that it is not good to marry to a rich man for the sake of educating ones children. The question is, do we choose to be born in poverty?

I believe that hard work will always pay. I have undergone a lot of peer pressure that has led some friends astray and they failed in education. I believe that copying bad behaviors of some girls will not take me anywhere in life and I am sure that my hard work in class will one day repay me. I urge girls to avoid copying what other girls do because of peer pressure because that can ruin their future. Peer pressure is high but set your goals higher because it is far better to suffer now so that in the future you will appreciate that you worked for a good cause.

Stay safe and live to bring good to your life, to that of your parents and of your family to be. Never look down upon yourself. I am a woman and I have the power to make a difference in my life. It is a choice which I made, and continue to make every day. I expect to model for generations to come that education is important, especially for females.

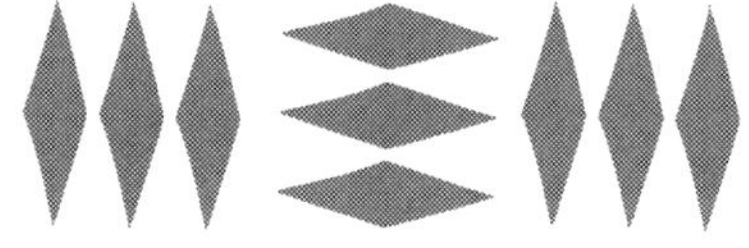

MY VOICE WILL BE HEARD

Madalitso R. Nkhonya

Madalitso R. Nkhonya is a Form 4 female student at Luwazi CDSS in Nkhata Bay District, Malawi. She is 22 years old and was born to her parents Tiwonge Kaonga and Rocky Nkhonya on 31 December 1995 in Chitipa district, which is the northernmost district in Malawi boarding Zambia. She is the second born in her family of 7 children, 3 girls and 4 boys. Their names, beginning form the oldest, are: Emmanuel, Madalitso, Zacharia, Edna, Rocky Jr. and the twins Patrick and Patricia. She is a Seventh Day Adventist and has lived in several districts in Malawi including Mzimba, Chitipa, Karonga and now Nkhata Bay. This has posed a number of difficulties for her. She wants to be a secondary school teacher or even the head teacher so she can help those going through similar problems.

Being too busy one can surrender and choose not to continue with their education or employment. What I know is that things become easier when one can divide their time. A person must have a good plan so I divide my time every day in order to overcome my struggles and to prevent the waste of time. I believe that time lost will never be regained.

I grew up in Malawi and it took me a long time to learn and know about myself. When I was younger and living with my parents I had to move around a lot due to various circumstances. I moved from Chitipa to Karonga District when I was small because my father had been transferred, then from Karonga to Mzimba District due to health problems and from Mzimba to Nkhata Bay District due to the transfer of my guardians. Moving so much caused me to repeat classes and fall behind my peers, and made me realize that wherever I go I needed to use my time effectively in order to make sure I kept moving forward.

Because I am the only girl at my guardian's home I am burdened with a lot of chores, drawing water from a distant borehole and carrying a full bucket of water on my head back home. I sweep in and around the house every morning and fetch and cut firewood for the house. I also cook the majority of the meals at home, like maize nsima which is our staple food in Malawi and relishes like masamba, beans and meat. I wash plates for everyone and wash my clothes by hand at the borehole once a week. I have to make sure I do these chores when needed because it is an important part of life in Malawi. These chores stop me from doing my school work and studying my notes. This is a barrier that I face every day. I know that in some areas and households this amount of work is not needed and allows people to concentrate on other things, like their education.

I completed my primary school at Gumi Primary School in Karonga. From there I was selected to Mlare Secondary School in Karonga. While I was in form 2 I had shortness of breath and was found to have asthma. which made me exhausted. As a result I failed to write my Junior Certificate of Education or JCE which would have allowed me to move on to Form 3. I had to repeat Form 2 instead of continuing onward but to help with my asthma issue, I was transferred to Nyungwe Secondary School also in Karonga District. Once there I was able to pass my exam and continue to Form 3. During that time I thought about not continuing with my education, due to my medical problem. My mom was the one encouraging me. She told me that education was the key to success and that I would feel better if I continued with my education and could find good employment. I would be stronger and be able to take care of myself and be independent.

My mother did not finish Secondary School and she wanted her first daughter to do well so I stayed in school and finished Form 3. As I was starting Form 4 I had an asthma attack which caused me to miss school, and again I transferred to another school, this time in Mzimba District. I was told that Mzimba's weather was better for me since it was cooler than Karonga and I may be able to breathe better, and it was true. During that time I stayed with my guardians, a pastor and his wife from the Seventh Day Adventist Church. I felt that once I finished my secondary education I could return to my home and family and attended Ezondwen Secondary School in order to finish Form 4. My health was good and I was doing well, but before I could finish, my guardians were transferred to Nkhata Bay District so once again I was transferred to my current school, Luwazi

Community Day Secondary School. Here I will finish Form 4 and my secondary education in July 2018. Even though Nkhata Bay district is also hot, my observation is that it is not as hot as Karonga so for now I am doing well.

As a female in Malawi I have faced some obstacles. My female friends have been married and some have children. There are those in my community who have asked me what am I waiting for, or why don't I get married. I tell them that life without education is nothing and that I want to know and learn as much as I can before I settle down and start a family. Sometimes I feel like my voice is not heard, and because I am young and female my words are not considered as much as a mans. This can be frustrating and makes me want to stay silent at times, but I cannot do that. I believe my voice will mean something to someone and I must continue to try so I can help those who need it.

My mother encouraged me to stay in school and I have found enjoyment in subjects like: English, Chichewa, Physical Science, Life Skills, Mathematics and Agriculture. Chichewa is Malawi's National Language, so it is an easy subject for me. Mathematics is needed if I plan on continuing to higher education and Life Skills is very important because it teaches me things that I can use every day in life as I chase my goals. I set goals and do not think of dreams because a goal is not just a fading dream, but something that I will achieve.

My goals begin with finishing my education and following the proper steps to become a teacher. As a teacher I will help my family, my community and my country. I want to provide an example for young girls in Malawi and Africa, so that they will see that it is possible to overcome the barriers we face every day. I want to advise my fellow young girls to continue their education and not give up. Just as my mother told me to continue I will be a voice to those who want to achieve their goals.

Inspired to Inspire. My Story

Dr. Maggie Madimbo

Dr Maggie Madimbo, is currently the Vice Chancellor for African Bible College in Lilongwe, Malawi. She did her PhD in Organizational Leadership Concentration Higher Education, Eastern University, Philadelphia, USA. Being born and raised in Malawi, Africa she knew what it means when people say their lives have been transformed. As an educator she has always rejoiced in witnessing the transformation of the people she teaches. She is persuaded that girls just like boys can excel in life. As an educator for the past 30 years she has seen how education has changed the destiny of many lives. Education is key to genuine transformation. She loves to mentor and inspire young people to dream big and think outside the box. She believes the potential that most girls have if well-developed is able to transform and change Malawi.

I am Dr Maggie Madimbo nee Sadyalunda. I come from Chiwaliwali village in Traditional Authority Kalumo, Ntchisi District. I am married to Mr Gilbert Madimbo of Traditional Authority Njobwa in Kasungu district. As a young girl I had mostly a happy childhood but there was a time when my dad lost his job and we had to go to the village and live a village life. My Dad lost his job when I was nine years old. Before he lost his job, he was at a managerial level so going to the village and living village life was a big change for us and it was not fun at all. In the village we had to continue with our education but at the same time we had to work in the garden as farmers to produce enough food for the family and to sell in order to have some income.

Village life was hard for me but I had to get used to it because it was the order of the day. During the week we had to go to school in the morning then proceed straight to the garden in the afternoon after classes. Throughout the growing season we mostly ate our lunch at the garden. Back in those days in the late 1970s there was little technology so that meant eating cold food (Nsima) every day for lunch. If you are familiar with Nsima you know that it tastes better when it is hot than when it is cold. Besides I do not enjoy cold foods so it was hard for me. It was during those difficult times in the village that I started dreaming of a different life style.

My ambition was to study hard and get out of the village life and live a different lifestyle. Going to the well to fetch water every day, carrying firewood on my head when coming from the garden and smearing the floors including toilet floors at school where the toilets were public and not well cared for was not fun for me. The only people who I saw leading a different life were mostly teachers. Of course, with my exposure when my dad was working I knew there were other jobs but I thought those were mostly for men. In my thinking women could only be school teachers or nurses. But all other nice jobs were for men.

After staying in the village for one year my older sister was selected to go to a boarding secondary school. As a result, I was the older girl in the home assuming most leadership roles in the kitchen. It was around the same time that my mother was sick and was admitted to Kamuzu Central hospital for close to 2 months. Life became even harder for me. It was during those hard moments that my dream was becoming clearer and clearer. I started desiring a profession that would take me out of village life. The hardships were so much that I even started thinking how I could make a difference in so many people's lives. As I write I can confidently say it is possible to have a better future even from a very humble background though it is not easy.

My goal was to get a job and live a better life. Back then I was convinced that I wanted to be a teacher. I always admired my teachers and I wanted to be like them. Mr Makonde my standard eight teacher was my favourite. I always wanted to be a school teacher like him. I knew that I enjoyed talking/teaching so I thought teaching would be ideal for me. Besides him when I was at Likuni Girls Secondary school I used to admire one of my teachers. Her name was Mrs Mulao and she was very tough. She played a very influential role in making me continue to admire the teaching job. Their joy and pride in teaching drew me closer to the teaching field. I like to talk and the teaching profession gives me the licence to do that. Now that I am a teacher I like it when I see my student grow and mature and continue to develop. My students' success feels like my own. I love to be part of good progress in other people's lives. I am proud to be a teacher. Teaching is a noble job. I enjoy it and I am smiling as I write this.

My proudest moment as a teacher is at the end of each school year at African Bible College when we have dinner organised in honour of the graduating class. During that time the graduates have a chance to share the highlight of their four year stay at college. It's so overwhelming for me to hear most of them saying I made a big difference in their lives. It feels good to hear that my labour is not in vain as a teacher. But then I did not want to be just any teacher. I had always dreamt of being a college professor and addressed as Dr Maggie Madimbo. I had a great dream but the means to get where I was to be was not clear because I did not get the right grades in form four. In a country where access to higher education institutions is limited I know that this dream could easily die a natural death. There were times when I felt like giving up my dream because I was not able to see the light at the end of the tunnel.

My back ground coming from a family where my dad was well educated but my mum was not was a barrier and a stepping stone at the same time. Growing up with a working dad made life very comfortable but when he lost his job everything changed. When my dad lost his job, it was difficult for us to cope with village life. Drawing water and cooking on an open fire were my biggest challenges. Then I always remember how in the village you kind of live in a glass house. Everyone knows everybody's business, there are no secrets. You could not have your own time for homework because everyone would expect you to be outside where other people were. Such a life makes it difficult to give your own family the best. That was certainly the challenge my family faced when we were in the village. I think the whole idea of uniformity makes it difficult for those who want to be above mediocrity. Because the general expectation is that everyone be at the same level.

In life I have learnt that we all need challenges to help us be uncomfortable enough to want change. For me when my father lost his job I realised that life was hard. I learnt some of the challenges that come with village life. My parents wanted us to realise that life in the village is difficult but education can get you out of that tough life. My parents chose to be different even in the village and that gave us children a good positive influence. They knew we were in the village but they never wanted us to end up as village girls and boys. They did not want to settle for the norm. Often my parents would discuss with us how they wanted the best for us. And my dad would always challenge us to be above where he had reached in life. My dad was always in some form of managerial positions and he had a college degree. When he found another job after three years in the village he started at the managerial level. So, as I was growing up I knew it was possible to be brought up in the village but not end up in the village. I was fully aware that my future was not so dependent on my past but how the future would be. It is important to acknowledge that God is the one who orders and establishes our plans. But it is also important always to have a dream and ask God to help you achieve your dream. This is so because if you aim at nothing you definitely hit it.

Now I want to talk about success. To me being successful is to be able to achieve beyond what one expected to achieve in life. In my case I started as a primary school teacher but now I am a Vice Chancellor for African Bible College. From a primary school teacher who had 40 points at MSCE to now being a PhD holder and a Vice Chancellor of an institution of higher learning is being successful.

God has been the force behind my success, I praise Him for that. Apart from God's hand and leading I think being hard working and having a clear vision has contributed to my being where I am today. Yes, I started as a primary school teacher but I knew from the word go that I would not end as a primary school teacher. In fact, my initial posting was an eye opener to me. I was trained as a primary school teacher but I was posted to teach at Kaluluma Community Secondary School and not to teach at a primary school. That said a lot to me. It made me realise the need for well qualified teachers but also it made me know that I can do better. I always visualized myself going farther with my education. In fact, when I was graduating with my masters I told myself not to buy the Masters' graduation gown because I wanted to have a PhD gown and cap. I am happy today that I own my PhD gown and hood. Vision is what pushes us to continue going even when the road ahead is not very clear.

In my journey to success I have had numerous challenges. My greatest challenge was when I went to Kenya for my Master's Degree. I was almost sent back home because I was a newly married young lady. As a woman I was not supposed to go to study while my husband was not studying. It was so strange for me to see the school administrator wanting to talk to my husband who was not their student but because he is a man and not me because I am a woman. I was not allowed to talk in that meeting and my husband had to decide whether to go back home or continue with my studies. I prayed that time for God's intervention and my husband was firm on his decision that I be given a chance to study. But the school demanded that my husband stay with me while I would be studying.

I praise God for Gilbert my husband because he has been very supportive. I went to a Christian University that was run by Life Ministry. In other countries it's called Campus Crusade for Christ. As a ministry they support families. They did not like married students to be separated while studying. Initially our plans were that I study while my husband would also be studying in Malawi.That was not accepted so we had to stay together in Nairobi, Kenya even though we had not initially planned and budgeted for that. So being a woman who admired to study at a University that was training Christian leaders for the African continent was a big challenge for me. Challenges make the journey tough but they do not make it impossible.

Education - My Life, My Pride, My Future

Matilda Phiri

Matilda Phiri is an award-winning Malawian author, model and entrepreneur. She holds a Bachelor of Social Science in Political Leadership with a minor in Social Work from Catholic University of Malawi. She was born on the 17th December, 1987 in Blantyre district and comes from Chiwembe village, T/A Kapeni. She is the first born in a family of two girls. She attended Nayizi and Misesa LEA School and Blantyre Secondary School.

Matilda started writing in 2005 when she was at Blantyre Secondary School (BSS). In 2011, she started publishing various articles, poems and short stories in local media in leading daily newspapers in Malawi. In 2013, she was given a column in Malawi news to publish her folktales every week. She still publishes her stories in local and international media. She has written movie scripts, radio plays, poems and short stories. Many of her stories are yet to be published and produced into movies. She has also worked with different organizations in Malawi such as the Centre for Social Research (CSR), National Statistical Office (NSO) and Invest in Knowledge (IKI) as a Social Researcher and survey Manager.

In 2015, Matilda became the first female to win an award in a Malawi Writers Union (MAWU) prestigious Peer Gynt Novel Competition with her story "Grace the Village Girl" and in 2017, she also won a prize in the MAWU/FMB Short Story Competition with a story titled "Smooth Operator." In 2018, she won again a prize in National Literary award with her book manuscript titled, "Bitter Lemonade."

Education is the key to my success and is my pride. I was born in Malawi in Blantyre district and I come from Chiwembe village, T/A Kapeni. I was born on 17th December, 1987, the first born in a family of two girls and was raised by a single mother after my parents divorced. I attended my primary education at Nayisi FP School before going to Misesa LEA School and Blantyre Secondary School.

I love school and will always love and support education because it has changed my life for the better. People may say that life begins at forty, but I say that education begins at secondary school then to college. I was selected to go to Soche Secondary School. Soche Secondary was a day school and I wanted a boarding school where I could concentrate on school only. Commuting to and from home to school has its disadvantage as I was distracted by things like television and found myself watching Nigerian movies which were famous during that time in 2002. It was the love of education that made me make the hard decision to leave home and movies to concentrate on school. I asked my mother to transfer me from a day school to a boarding school and I secured a place at Blantyre Secondary School. I smile as this was one of my long time wishes and it was a dream come true to be accepted at a national boarding school. This was in 2002 and I was still young, at 14 years old.

On the day that I arrived at Blantyre Secondary School I was welcomed by hungry young boys who were sexually active such that they found me attractive and tried whatever they could to win me. I knew that if I smiled at them my future dream would not be realized and vowed never to bow down to their sexual desires for the sake of my anticipated bright future. The boys both in Form 1 to 4 wanted my attention and wanted to date me. Some boys who came to propose love to me were boys in their early twenties and even some in their early thirties. I was young, and I didn't want boys. For what? I wanted school, and I came to a boarding school to concentrate on my studies.

I wanted to be a pilot and the answer that I had for all the boys coming to date me was, "No. I'm still young. I don't know what you're telling me. I don't want you." I was not even saying that I was sorry, because I was not wrong. I remember this starting even when I was in Primary school. I used to receive letters from boys and I would tear them up. My mother had also told me not to play with boys when I become of age (started menstruation). She said that boys could ruin my future and run away from responsibility once I fall pregnant. I grew up appreciating that unplanned babies are not easy to care for and only adults can manage them. I was too young for a baby.

In 2003, I joined Students Christian (SCOM) a fellowship praying organization for students where they told us the truth of dating. I still remember it very well, the strong message which helped me to finish my education without any disturbance from boys. The message was that dating when you're in school is a sin before God because you're still young. We were advised that there will be a time when we are at college when we can start dating as we prepare ourselves to get married. Dating is only accepted by God when you want to get married, you want to know the person who you wish to marry and do not involve sex because it is a sin. I understood these powerful words and trusted them. Because I received good advice from prayer gatherings, I made the decision not to date any boy until I completed my secondary education. I trust that since I did not waste my precious time dating boys, and never dated any boy throughout all my secondary school life, I managed to pass with good Malawi school certificate of education grades.

One time at Blantyre Secondary School in 2004 I nearly gave up because of a false report that I was involved in a school disorder. There was a school strike whereby the students revolted against the new school rules, low education and meal standards. The students were tired, and they told the school officials their concerns, but the situation did not improve. This resulted in students being bored and resorted to destroying school property like windows and doors. I did not join those that were looting school property but was running away from classes to the hostel while some students started breaking windows. One of my teachers saw me running and thought I was also throwing stones and yet I was not.

The following day, we heard that they had closed the school and that it will be communicated through radio when we should report back to school. All of the students were told to leave the school that same day and I went home. I felt bad that I was losing learning time because I liked school. After 3 weeks had passed we heard on radio that we should report back to school the following week with the exception of 18 students who were identified as ring leaders of the stampede. These were commanded to pay back the cost of the damages to the school for repairs.

Indeed, the students' parents shouldered the costs of repairing the school which was K2500 each. This was a lot of money as some parents expressed they struggled to pay school fees and this was an added burden. My mother lamented at my perceived behavior although I had not taken part in the scandal. It was a big blow to me and I was very heart broken. I was angry with my school and teachers, especially the teacher who claimed that he saw me take part in the vandalism and included mine in the names of people who started the strike. How could I go back to such a school and how will I see them? Would I concentrate in class seeing this teacher in front of me? If I don't go back to this school, where else will I go? This was the best national school near Blantyre, my hometown. I had so many questions in my mind and considered calling it quits but my mother consoled me and advised me to avoid bad company before she sent me back to school. I realized that bygones are bygones and that to err is human and to forgive is divine.

My mother is working class and has always been a strong woman and managed to take care of her children through her work as a clerk officer. I knew she was able to manage us because of her education or she couldn't have made it. We could have lived in dire poverty because my father went to South Africa and neither helped nor supported us. Knowing this about education, I went back to school where we were welcomed by a stiff punishment, tasked to construct a road on the campus. We had already lost some lessons and lost another week while our friends went on learning but I knew that one day I would forget these pains and rejoice at my success in school. I trusted that I would not be let down despite that I had missed quite a number of days without learning.

After all the punishments, I was back in class and got all the notes that my friends learnt, managed to pick up everything I had missed and was ready to write my Malawi School Certificate of Education (MSCE). I thank God because I passed very well, went on to university to further my studies and graduated with a degree in Political Leadership with a minor in Social Work. I was happy that I did not get pregnant because I had the dream of completing school before engaging in a sexual relationship.

In 2006 I wrote a book called "Grace the Village Girl," which retold some of the events that I faced during my secondary education and I have now published the book and am selling it. I must admit that the proceeds from the books sale are giving me more money than I had ever dreamt of. I am able to pay my own bills and buy whatever I want, and it's because of education. If not for my education, I would never have known how to write a book.

Today, I am a multiple award winning Malawian author, model and an entrepreneur. I was already a millionaire at the age of twenty seven years because of hard work and a clear focus on my chosen path, to further education plus the writing career which I cherish. With my Bachelor of Social Science degree, I have worked with different organizations as a researcher and survey manager and earn money through writing competitions that I enter and win. I am proud of my success and achievement, and look forward to more success stories. I don't depend on any man but solely my businesses, because of school and my education. I claim that education is my life, my pride and my future.

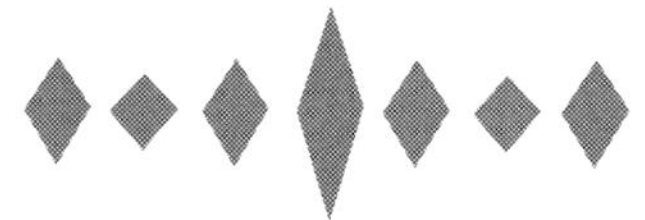

My Mother, My Anchor

Maureen Mlenga

Mercy Maureen Mlenga (nee Matiya) is a bonafide Malawian Senior Citizen who lives at Chibwana village T.A.Kuntaja, Chilomoni Blantyre and works for Universal Industries as Production Manager. Mercy went to secondary school at Malosa where she endured and completed Form Four, despite family financial challenges and became the first female Assistant Manager at Pharmanova, a Pharmaceutical Company.

Her first short story 'Just in Time' was published in 1987 in Malawi News. Maureen continues to write and has at various writing activities rubbed shoulders with the likes of Professor David Rubadiri, Wokomaatani Malunga, Willie Zingani, Afred Msadala, Hoffman Aipira, Zondiwe Mbano, Sambalikagwa Mvona, Edward Chitsulo, Janet Karim and Emily Mkamanga. Moreover, she has been invited to write and recite her poems by Zhara Nuhru at their conferences when she was UNDP representative in Malawi. I recall that I have recited my own works locally and in Tswane South Africa at a SADC multidisciplinary gathering.

Maureen has served as a board member at Mudi SACCO, World Hope International and Claim Mabuku. Her strive to attain and struggle for education as a girl child compels her to promote girls to stay in school and not rush for early marriages. She gives motivational talks to girls at schools like Likhubula Primary School in Chilomoni.

Maureen has a strong passion for nurturing young children and youth to become strong Christians. She composes and teaches songs to Sunday School children, authored a Chichewa Book in a project by Claim Mabuku to sensitize young school children on HIV/Aids and donated some copies at this local school. Further to that she is involved in nurturing Sunday School Children at Local Church Likhubula Evangelical Church to be better Christian citizens and also coordinates Church Youth Activities. She enjoys writing in the vernacular to reach out to everyone despite their education (considering illiteracy rate in Malawi is still high). She also writes in Yao – her mother's language - to reach out to them as well.

She loves singing for the Lord and is currently a member of Blantyre Joint Choir.

I woke when the Angelus Bell chimed. I woke up and began reciting the three Hail Mary prayers. This was a daily activity at Malosa Secondary School. If anyone defied the order or was found walking after the bell had rung they were severely punished. As a Form One girl I had gotten used to following instructions to the letter. On this morning although I was reciting the prayer, my mind was in turmoil for the Headmaster Mr. Lees had summoned us to his office. There were about twenty of us and in his usual tradition he cleared his throat before addressing us.

"The Bursar brought me a list of your names regarding non payment of school fees. Have any of you got a valid reason for not paying your fees?"

There was dead silence in the jam packed office. You could hear a pin drop.

"Alright, since you all don't have any reasons for not paying your fees, you can leave my office, go to your dormitories, collect the fees and give them to the Bursar. Only then can you go back to attend classes, otherwise no way."

"But Sir, forgive us...we don't..." we all spoke in unison.

"Silence!" Mr. Lees banged his wooden table, "I asked a simple question which you failed to answer. How come you have now found your voice? Get out of my office."

We rushed out of the office murmuring. Having been raised by a single mother, in my secondary school days, to get school fees let alone transport money from Blantyre to school was a tall order. In my primary school days I had been my dad's pride in 1964 at Kachingwe Primary School in Chiladzulu. In total, seven students were selected to go to secondary school and I was the only girl in the group.

All was well for a while until my father was forced to go on a self imposed exile in fear of the political situation then. Dad was not a politician but a civil servant - a health assistant at Zomba General Hospital, but had very good connections with Henry Masauko Chipembere and other Cabinet Ministers of that era who were considered vying to overthrow the government. So when the 1964 Cabinet Crisis threatened, even close friends of the fired Ministers, including my dad's life was at risk as the Malawi Youth Leaguers and Malawi Young Pioneers who were acting as law enforcers that time were baying for his blood.

This was a bad blow to our family's survival as the bread earner had to leave Malawi for an unknown destination just to save his own life. There was no way we could communicate with him to get any financial support for family upkeep, let alone my school fees. Mum was a full-time housewife and though she engaged in small businesses to make ends meet, it was too much for her to fend for five children with two of us at secondary school.

Finally, my sister Victory had to withdraw from school to help mum bake and sell doughnuts for our daily sustenance. My dad had some property, a maize mill and herds of cattle and goats, but they were all looted by evil men when they heard that he had fled the country. Mum had to leave my father's village and went back to her father's place in Blantyre. That's where I found her after being chased back from school to collect school fees.

"Mercy my daughter, there's no money in the house, even just for a little porridge flour for your two year old brother here. How do you think I can raise five pounds sixteen shillings for your school fees?"

I well understood my mother's predicament. I wished there was a way I could get the money without putting her into any form of debt. I spent part of the night crying and trying to dream how I she could make it possible. I was craving to return to school so I could realise my dream of becoming an air hostess.

When I woke up the next day my mother was not around. My elder sister Victory told me that she had left at cockcrow with my elder brother Solomon, but they did not inform her where they had gone.

They came back by noon looking tired, exhausted and hungry. Their faces were long and I knew I was causing more havoc to the already suffering family. Mum reported that she had walked three kilometers with my brother in search of money from a distant relative. When this issue of lack of school fees was reported to my uncle who was staying in the same village, he brushed this aside as nonsense.

"Why waste your time with this girl child? Just let her be. If by any luck you get money you better invest in the education of these boys. Remember she will soon get married and her husband will take care of her. But, it does not matter if she can't get married. She can become a tailor. That trade doesn't need education, does it? After all there are so many illiterate tailors around."

I cried bitterly thinking that was going to be the end of my school since in our culture, uncles have the final say in their sister's children. However, to my surprise my mother stood her ground and announced that she was sending me back to school so that I can bring a change in our family and the community. My uncle's eyes turned red and he looked at my mother with a wrinkled face. He spat on the ground, rose and stormed out of our house seething.

I felt sorry for my mum for when I looked at her, tears were trickling down her haggard face, but she assured me she could do everything possible to send me back to school.

Within the week I observed mum's face was all smiles as she sung her favourite song. I later realised she was successful to source my fees. It materialised after the distant relative she had visited loaned her just enough for the fees.

I was all smiles as I packed my suitcase to return to school. Since there wasn't even money for transport, my other uncle who worked at the Post Office, offered to take me to school on his motorcycle. I was delighted by the kind gesture though I feared I would be ridiculed by my school mates, so I requested my uncle to drop me a few metres before our school gate.

I went back to school with renewed confidence for I had vowed to make my mother proud. I didn't indulge in any of the activities that could ruin my education. I stayed away from the Friday school dances because I had no smart dress to put on, neither did I ever go to the market at Namwera turn off because I didn't have any money to spend. I appreciated my needy situation and respected my mother's efforts such that I resolved to persevere. I sat for my junior certificate, passed and went into Form Three.

There was one friend whom I called a Good Samaritan, Flonney Itimu Gallanje, who played big sister to me. She shared whatever groceries her parents brought her and took me to her home in Zomba during school holidays.

I didn't have transport money to take me home. I prayed and advised that we should work hard in class. Yes, she had to remain in school for I felt she was God - sent to open arms to my relief and I will forever be indebted to her. Now she is late, may her soul rest in peace.

Next surprise was a letter which mum sent me.

"My dear daughter, I have come to a standstill. You appreciate that I have singlehandedly tried to allow you complete your education. But, I want to tell you that much as I would have loved that I continue supporting you, I am only being honest to let you know that I can no longer manage to pay your fees and support our family. I look forward to seeing you back home when your headmaster next chases you back.

"But why mum, after all we have been through, why give up now? Do you want me to be a tailor as your brother suggested?" I cried.

"No, my daughter. Remember that day I escorted you to Wenela bus depot, I felt pity to see your fellow students elegantly dressed. On top of that they carried plenty of food packs while you only carried this suitcase. No dear daughter, I don't want you to remain a laughing stock at your school. I believe that when you return home, your junior certificate will qualify you to find something worthwhile as a job."

I gathered courage, wrote her back, vowing I wasn't leaving school until I sit for my Cambridge Examinations in the next three years. As for my poverty, I would trust God to see me through. I folded the letter in a khaki envelope and posted to her.

Indeed, I persevered and mum continued cooking doughnuts for my fees, until I finally completed my Cambridge Examinations. Though I didn't do very well, I passed well enough such that I was on reserve list waiting to be enrolled at Soche Hill College Entrance. However, while waiting the next luck, I applied and secured a job with Nzeru Radio Manufacturing Company. I opted for the job and I was then able to relieve mum and my sister in taking care of our family.

A year later I met the love of my life, Alec Mlenga, then a salesman with Phillips Distribution Company. We got married and were blessed with four children. At some point I resigned after I got my next employment opportunity with Pharmanova Pharmaceutical Company as a production clerk, then promoted to supervisor, then another promotion to an assistant production manager.

I was the first woman to hold that position in that company.

As I worked to my best performance, I rekindled my passion for writing which dated back to my school days when I was a reporter for Malosa Bits & Pieces, which was our weekly newsletter, and Cholinga (Aim) the school magazine. Further to that I enrolled for French lessons at French Cultural Centre in Blantyre City to an advanced level. Next I enrolled for secretarial studies at the Polytechnic and studied up to intermediate level.

Amidst all these busy engagements and as a mother and wife I used to write short stories for Malawi News and Nation Newspaper, wrote poems for Kwathu Drama Group, the number one drama group in Malawi then.

My mum passed on to glory on 18th August 2016 but I have her to thank for what I am today. She will always occupy a special place in my heart. I still embrace her for her brevity against my uncle's decision to chuck me out of school. She is my loving model who defied our cultural norms and practices then which did not value education for the girl child. She invested in me and she will remain my heroine as she was my anchor whose shoulders I leaned upon to attain my successes in life.

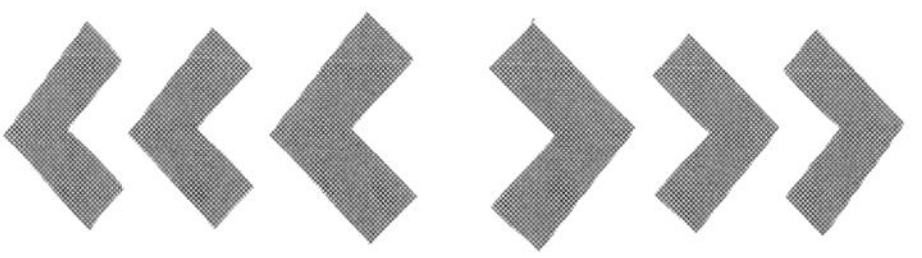

Desired Goal

Mphatso Major

Mphatso is a girl aged 18, she started school at the age of 4. During her early childhood she wanted to be a pilot but she changed after one of her friends discouraged her. He said women were not allowed to be pilots because it was meant for men. As time passed, she was absorbed in journalism. To her, that was the only way she could have changed some things that seemed undesirable to her. For this reason, she was trying her best to reach her destination. But things were not easy. The outcome was parallel to her expectations. Starting from her community, huge number of girls were married and it was really difficult to find role models. The worst thing to her was that she did not want to get married before she achieved her dream. As such, this gives her courage to be one of the fabulous ladies in her community. Motivating others, encouraging, inspiring as well as being a role model that's what makes her be a hard worker. To her even though she was poor it should not be a barrier to achieve what she wants. She doesn't want others to suffer simply because she did not work hard at a certain point. As I'm talking now I'm a student at Polytechnic studying social science in community development.

It was only questions and memories that boosted my head, the pain remain deep inside my heart stirring my anger. I couldn't believe this, for the first time, I wished I could have not exist in this world. Thinking about my future what kind of a woman I'm I going to be, an achiever, a failure, or what. Not even a single answer found what else can I do. The main reason was my biological makeup. I had no choice and it was really a baffling situation. On top of that my parents were expecting a lot from me and I realize that if I will fail to achieve and bear notable branches in me, my siblings will fail as well because I denote as an example to them.

It put me under pressure to work day and night coming up with innovative ideas and concentrate much on my studies. Though things where like this,

I was occupied in many professions being a journalist, a lawyer, a farmer, a business lady as well as social worker. Honestly, I do not feel comfortable on issues that affect vulnerable people, less privileged and girls. From the bottom of my heart I want to help those who cannot defend themselves. I have a great passion on this because I've been staying in a community where the youth were not given a chance to participate in a community development. What they know is violence. It took me a couple of years to write about this from the power and motivation I gain from VoiceFlame I'm no longer afraid. Praise and thanks to you Jehovah for making this time in my life.

The journey begun without knowing where exactly I was going with my education. Things were no longer the same. I lacked financial support because my father was not working at that time. I was looking after my siblings at home, while my parents were far away doing some work in search of money to support the family. I started losing hope and it was painful seeing myself failing to achieve my goals. Some days I even went to school with an empty stomach and concentration as well as participation in class was poor. I was really worried about my future. I started excluding myself from friends. This affect me negatively and I remember I lose weight and I was no longer the same Mphatso I use to know. I was staying in hiding and quiet places.

Since I felt too much heavy for my own body simply because I was much stressed up. I was considered myself as failure and I was shy to answer questions in class. I didn't share my challenge to anyone because I thought there was no one who can help. It reach to the extent that I started suffering from ulcers due to too much stress, but I was not aware.

One day as I was crossing the road, I didn't check all directions and I remember it was worries, fears and stress that filled my mind. The bicycle was coming from my right side. He was about to hit me. Fortunately the other man pushed me in the other side. That was how I was saved but it could have been such terrible accident.

At school I go straight to the tap, I was too much thirsty. Upon reaching the tap, I found one of the workers, he looked at me closely and asked what troubled me. In his question it shows that upon seeing me, my face tells sad story. I lied nothing happened. He advised me that I should stop stressing myself because I can end up making wrong decisions. He was saying the truth but I couldn't take it due to the situation I was in. In class my performance dropped, reaching to the point that one of my teachers criticized me in public. I failed his subject and he gave me punishment. This was adding a salt on fresh wound. I felt sorry to myself and ashamed in front of my friends.

On this day, one of our teachers announced about a new club and only girls were allowed to join. This club was called VoiceFlame and it was based on writing and reading. The main purpose was to empower girls to develop the spirit of writing which help them to diffuse fears, stress and build self confidence. I remember it was wonderful moment in my life being the first girl to join VoiceFlame. I still get surprised up today what forced me to be one of writers, because I was not interested to join clubs at school, but I know it was God's plan so that I can reach my destiny.

My first meeting with Chikondi is still remarkable up to today and I learnt a lot from her. For the first time I saw some light penetrating deep inside my heart, which was filled with total darkness over. From a sudden my body was overwhelmed after I heard a voice from this lady to write five positive things about ourselves. It looks simple now but that time I swear I did not know what should I write, since at that time I lacked creativity.

By command I wrote but I did not read because was afraid to stand in front of my friends. It all happened because I was lacking self awareness which is the main challenge among the girls. It took me much time to discover exactly who am I. It was VoiceFlame that open my mind, rise my self esteem and my confident. This gives me a room as a writer to express my voice freely. Our voice is a powerful painkiller that heals a wound.

In Malawi we have all the possibilities of bringing change and transform our country. But this can happen if we change our negative mind. Girls stay positive, know yourself, desist the spirit of accepting problems. Let's use minor things that we have to move forward and achieve what we want in life. Remain in silence will just add problems in our everyday life, our voice is a powerful tool to break boundaries, see new opportunities and progress in life.

Education Hardships Passed

Olgha Sheha

Mrs Olgha Sheha Saidi was born on 1st February, 1953 and is now 65 years old. She was born in rural Nyasaland, now Malawi, in Nsanje district in the Southern region of Malawi, which was then Port Herald. She was born at Chimtedza village, TA Mlolo, in the Chiromo area. Her father was polygamous, married six wives of which her mother was the fifth. In her mother's house she was the first born of five children, four girls and one boy. In total, the compound of her father and the six wives had twenty children, fourteen girls and six boys. To him, Olgha was number twelve.

Olgha attended various primary schools due to lack of education facilities and inadequate teachers. She did her secondary school education at Providence Girls Secondary School in Mulanje, Southeastern part of Malawi, from 1971 to 1974. Then she went for a secretarial course at Mpemba Staff Training College from 1976-1977. After that she worked as a secretary at various ministries-Agriculture, Social Welfare, Health, Registrar General, Information, Legal Aid, Tourism, Bunda College of Agriculture among others. She also studied for a diploma in community development and business management. Now she is self employed at Environmental and Educational Resources and Development Trust, a Non-Governmental Organization (NGO) which she founded. The mission statement of the NGO is to eradicate poverty, empower women and provide literacy programs.

Olgha comes into writing through an interest that developed in order to put her thoughts on paper. Little by little she started getting more interested such that she has written various development related articles one of which was sent to the Food and Agriculture Organization.

There was no one who was educated in our clan, such that I had no model but, I got to know that education is important. That is why I stood and walked with courage and determination, defying the unfortunate environment in which I grew up until I took home a Malawi Certificate of Education. It was only later that people in our village started to accept that if I, a girl had managed to complete secondary school, why can't their girls make it too?

My father was Mr. Ngwale Sheha. In those colonial days and by African standards he was a rich man who was envied by many in our lower Shire district of Nsanje. He had plenty of livestock, cattle, goats, sheep and poultry. He was also a fisherman with fishing nets in Mangochi, Nsanje and Chikwawa. He owned three maize mills and employed labor to assist him run his business empire. Polygamy in our Sena culture is very common, such that my father married six wives. My mother was the fifth.

Our village had no school but the Indian shop owners who wanted their children to be educated sent their children to town, either Blantyre or Limbe, where there were schools. My father seemed to have had value for education such that he arranged with an elder of a church to teach the children in our village. They had agreed on a fee which was paid by the end of each month and my father constructed a grass thatched shelter for us.

There were four classes. Sub A, Sub B, then Standard one and two. When a school pupil passed from Standard three to four, we had to walk three miles to a religious school which was a bit farther from this local school. For those who could not manage to travel to that distant school this marked the end of their formal education. Fortunately for me, my mother was a traditional beer brewer (Kabanga). She bought a bicycle for me and I learned cycling so that I was able to continue with my education at the distant school.

My parents registered me at another school when I reached standard five and I went to stay with one of my step mothers in the compound because it was closer to the school than my mother's home. Within a short stay I realized I was being sent to do several domestic chores such as fetching for water, going to the maize mill and fetching firewood. I could hardly find time to concentrate on school assignments and sometimes missed classes. I found it hard to give enough time to my education. But I did not give up. I had to wake up very early, do house work, bathe in cold water and rush to school.

One year the Indian community mobilized themselves and constructed a school for their children in the village. Upon liaising with the minister of education they saw this as an opportunity to construct an integrated school which later accommodated both African and Indian children. As soon as I heard about this opening I thought it wise to go back and stay with my biological mother. I sighed in relief because the Lord answered my prayer to be rescued from the violence I was going through. When Malawi gained independence from the colonial rule in 1964 the school was upgraded to full primary school where classes were constructed up to standard eight, which is the highest class at primary school in Malawi.

My face beamed with profound joy in 1970 when standard eight results had my name as one selected to a boarding school at Providence Secondary school. This joy was short lived when I started observing that my stepsisters stopped coming close to me. I later realized it was because they did not make it to secondary school. They were not happy that I was excelling in education and I heard my sisters and brothers murmur that I was taking more of my father's wealth by going to school. They told my father that I should not continue with school. Then some of these sisters were either married or impregnated while in primary school

By this time I was grown up and matured such that I was said to be delaying the start of taking care of a man and bearing children. My father was in favour of my relative's suggestion such that he advised me to stop going to school but I declined and clung to school. Then my father told me that he was done with me so I had no one to pay school fees for me.

He told me straight, "If you want to continue going to school then tell your mother to do that." He even directed my mother to stop beer brewing, claiming that he was a Muslim and his wife should not be engaging in the beer business. My mother obeyed because she said if she continued it would be a sign that she did not obey my father and that would lead to my father terminating the marriage. Since my father was the bread winner she would be laughed at for disobeying her husband.

I still wanted to go to school, so in order to have a source of income for school fees and other expenses, I secretly started brewing beer which was sold by my neighbors who then gave me the proceeds. Our neighbor trained me how to brew this type of beer. It was a big risk because I had to stay awake late at night to sell from the neighbor's house because my father was a Muslim and could not allow beer at our house. Some even wanted a place to sleep. I had to endure this as my aim was to complete my secondary education then find out what I would do next. I didn't want to just stay or get married, doing school was my pleasure. I also did other small businesses like frying fish and making doughnuts. When I went up to Form Two I realized my mother could no longer afford to support me, so I started distilling spirits (locally known as kachasu) which I sold myself during the holidays. My father did not know where I was getting the fees but one day told me, "Since you are still going to school, make sure you pass. If you fail your Junior Certificate this mother of yours will have to pay me back what I have spent on your school since you started."

Two years later I passed my Junior Certificate Examination and went into Form Three. Life became tougher when my father divorced my mother because she was the one encouraging me to continue with education. I was grown up to him such that I should have been married. I endured the situation all along while my sisters and father were on one side, against me continuing with school until I completed Form Four and passed my MSCE.

I secured a job at a local import and export company in Blantyre but within the workplace there arose more trouble because I refused to have sexual intercourse with the Operation's Manager. Within the year I was dismissed on false allegations but continued on another search for my next chance of employment. I got another job within the same year when I managed to secure employment as a clerk with a government agricultural division. This time the earning was very fair such that I started paying school fees for my little brothers and sisters who were also ignored by our father. God continued to favor me as I applied and did a secretarial course, after which I worked as a secretary in different departments and government institutions. I did not give up in all of the efforts that I had put my heart into. I was a rolling stone.

Alongside working I started doing a cross border business such that I commuted between Malawi and Mozambique. When my manager discovered that I was doing business in addition to the work I was doing at his workplace he wrote me a letter of dismissal.

I was conscious I was fast losing my work career as I was being hindered by circumstances so I gave up totally and applied to do Community Development which I studied up to advanced diploma, a level which was rarely attained by girls in those days. I wished that I had gone further to do a degree course but could not because of lack of finances. I am the only one that completed my education as a woman in our family. My sister did not complete because my father passed on in 1980 and the property was shared among all children. The young in our family, the fourth and fifth born were given a cow each but they all failed.

As am now growing old, at sixty five years I registered an organization and my vision is to eradicate poverty, empower women, youth and vulnerable people. I know God has deposited wisdom in me, such that I believe that if given the chance and a better environment, I will continue to contribute to reducing Malawi poverty and illiteracy so that the many youths who remain unemployed might be helped to become productive citizens.

My Story

Prudence Kalako

Prudence Kalako is one of the youngest managers at one of Malawi's leading tobacco buying and processing companies, Japan Tobacco International (JTI) in the country's capital city of Lilongwe. Before her current job, she worked for the government of Malawi as a Women's Programmes Officer where she was mainstreaming gender, HIV/AIDS and other women related issues in agricultural projects. Prudence holds a Bachelor of Science Degree in Agricultural Economics and is currently studying towards a master's degree in International Management. She is also an aspiring writer who has attended VoiceFlame's writing workshops.

Do we all remember what our ambition was when we were young? I do. Because this is one of the most common questions a lot of children are asked. In Malawi, where I am from, a lot of kids are asked not only how old they are, but what they want to work as when they grow up. There is actually specific facts that a child needs to memorize in anticipation of being asked by elders and there is joy that the elders show when they respond so impressively. I simply cannot forget the feeling of satisfaction every time I could respond to that cliché of a question – my response was always the same – "when I grow up I want to be a banker".

Growing up, my ambition was to work in a bank. I did not know what a banker did, nor did I know what would be required for me to be one, but yet that was what I wanted to become. It was not the most common of career ambitions to have. I wanted to be a banker because I had an amazing role model, my mother, Joyce. Her name resonated with her personality. She was always full of joy and brought joy to many people. She, at the time, worked in a bank and I was her biggest fan. All I knew was that when I grew up I wanted to be like her. She was a single woman raising 3 kids. She did this so gracefully that I cannot imagine how hard it must have been during that time. She was beautiful and always bubbly.

I was always a smart and competitive child. My family was and still is my strongest support system. I always made sure to make it to the top three of the class. This continued to be my trend throughout primary school. I would always get some award at the end of the year for my good performance. I worked hard because I knew I wanted a better life for myself, my mother and the rest of my family. Unfortunately, my mother did not live long enough to witness my success. She died just as I completed my primary education. So, there I was, a smart eleven year old, heartbroken with the loss of my mother and role model.

If you are from Africa you understand the concept of extended families. My siblings and I were split between two families. I got into one of my mother's older sister's family who raised me like her own daughter, constantly pushing me to do better. Of course, it helped that she was a teacher by profession. I was fortunate enough to get into a good Catholic secondary school. My aunt made sure my afternoons were filled with school work. I remember how she would always ask if I had completed all my assignments. If I did, she would tell me it was not enough, and that I needed to go and study. I slowly got into the habit of studying and got motivated even more to maintain my trend if I wanted to attain my goals.

I managed to uphold my trend of good performance and got selected to a government university and qualified for an education loan. This brought me so much relief as I did not want my family to struggle with the burden of having to source funds for school fees anymore. By this time, I had changed my career goal - I no longer wanted to be a banker. I wanted to be more. As I grew up with the 'banker' ambition, people would encourage me to work hard at mathematics. I did work extra hard at it and got really good at it. At this point I had grown up and had a clearer picture of what I wanted my success to look like. My 'grown-up' ambition was now to be an economist.

It was not the easiest thing to maintain my good performance throughout college. Here I was in college and for the first time away from home. With so much freedom I no longer had my aunt by my side to remind me to do my assignments or to remind me to study. This time I had to do it all on my own. College is fun, we all know it, You can do almost anything you want with your time. With this much freedom, it would be very easy to fail. However, I still had the routine of being top of the class, so I made sure not to break it.

First year was our general year. I still had not qualified for the economics course but I was determined to make it so I studied even harder, interacted with those outstanding, intelligent people in class who always had a ready answer to everything that was raised by the lecturers. By second year I made it into my dream course. I was going to become an economist! All my hard work was finally starting to show off and I was going to make my family proud. Unfortunately, my aunt also did not live long enough to see me through college but passed away during my first year in college. I was devastated. Why did the universe keep taking away the people who saw the potential in me to become a successful woman?

I completed my college studies and graduated with a degree in Economics with a credit. It was a big achievement as there were only a few of us in our class with such an outstanding grade. It did not take long for me to find a job. My first job did not really give me the opportunity to use all the knowledge I had acquired and was so eager to use. Luckily, I found the job I am in currently. The first two years in my current job were not easy as I was and I still am, in a male dominated industry where I constantly need to prove that I am the right person for the job and can do it well. I maintained my focus and ensured that I delivered on all tasks assigned. I was given the same tasks as my male colleagues. Do not get me wrong, I am not complaining but must say that being a woman did not make this easy. But, I made it, six years down the line. I have gained the respect of both my company and the industry. I can confidently say that the management team in the company has all the confidence in my work. I am living my dream career.

My ultimate goal in life is to contribute to young girls' confidence in their own paths to success. Everything is possible and every career can be achieved. As girls, we should not see obstacles as a block but as motivation to strive for whatever we would like to become.

Search For My Destiny

Rhoda Zulu

Rhoda Zulu was born on 10 December 1960 and hails from Kanjovu Village in Golomoti, Traditional Authority Kachindamoto in Dedza district. She went to Likuni Girls' Secondary School and Lilongwe Teachers' College before entering Domasi College of Education for a Diploma in Education. She retired early, joined broadcasting at the Malawi Broadcasting Corporation (MBC) where she initiated Mai Wamakono (Modern woman). Currently works with the Story Workshop Education Trust (SWET), a local Non-Governmental Organization in Malawi, which deploys Social and Behavior Change Communication.

Rhoda has a drive and value for education and did her post-secondary education after she got married, and is currently studying for Masters in Behavior Change and Communication at the Malawi Polytechnic in Blantyre and lives in Blantyre in South Lunzu, Area 12, Machinjiri.

She enjoys reading and writing, accessed capacity building by the Malawi Writers' Union as well as FEMRITE Uganda Women Writers. She writes short stories, features and poetry. One of her stories published by Uganda Women Writers, "Summoning the Rains," sets deep in an African village where Namapeta, a village girl is forced into initiation and soon drops out of school curtailed by her mother, Mai Nini. She was hastily prepared for marriage through initiation, thereby cutting short her ambition of becoming a nurse. Soon family conflict, complicated by the failure to bear children led in desperation to her accepting sexual cleansing by an African doctor, and later the death of her husband due to constant fights. Unfortunately, Namapeta was accused of killing the man.

Currently Rhoda is an active member of PEN International, Malawi Chapter, Poetry Association of Malawi, a founding member of the African Network for Women Writers, a contributor to a women's forum, www.makewana.com and has contributed to organizing secondary school girls' writing competitions and young women writers' compilations like The Grafted Tree and other stories, This Small World.

My name is Rhoda Nyundo Zulu. I am an ambitious, dynamic and progressive woman. I am aware that great people we admire are ordinary people just like you and me, only that they have a special drive, determination and desire (Developing the Leaders around You by John Maxwell). According to the Oxford Advanced Learners' Dictionary, University Press 2002, to succeed is to achieve what you've been trying to get or to be victorious. Hence, I am on a pilgrim's journey, towards my own uniqueness. So, if you think that you are done in by any failure, then this essay is tailor made to inspire you.

When my mum was expecting me, my father was hoping for a boy, so though I was born a female, he still named me Harvey (meaning warrior), but I was christened Rhoda. One day I asked him why he called me Harvey and he said, "Our culture values a boy such that he is given charge of a family clan. This is one reason why although I grew up as an orphan in various families I still went further with school. Now I am a father but I soaked my legs in a pail of water to remain awake and study. Your mother was denied further education by her own father who opted for her brother, yet the brother failed. I will give you all my energy, so you can excel though you are a girl."

I appreciated his determination as I wondered what was special about males. When I started standard one my teacher was female, Mrs Gomile. When I fell sick I was fascinated by a female nurse who treated me. In view of the nurse I admired the nurses uniform, especially the white head cap. By and by, these role models inspired me to work hard and in 1975 I was selected to Likuni Girls Secondary School and was surprised by my father's reward, "Learn to drive this Raleigh bicycle. I await to see you drive a vehicle one day as I do."

While at Likuni Girls" School there were several career talks by women that were educated and were employed. Aim High, Never Tire was the school slogan of encouragement. Regrettably, back home my relationship with my father turned sour after I only passed Malawi School Certificate of Education Exams. By not making it to university I failed to envisage any light beyond my failure. I was a shame even to our teachers since nobody was selected from our class.

My father called me loud, "Harvey! Why did you fail? Your headmistress Sister Perpetua Zitande assured me you were university material."

I looked down and left. "Why has Aim High, Never Tire failed to prove my success?"

All along I'd put maximum effort on my studies to please my father. Maybe I was complacent after mock exams listed me on top ten. I wiped out my tears and clenched my hands, "This failure is not permanent," I consoled myself.

One day a friend of mine, Jane from Ntcheu visited us. She too, just like me, had only passed without getting selected to university. She sought permission from my parents that I should accompany her to Lilongwe, but I was surprised when she led me to her boyfriend, who then brought me his friend to get married to.

I refused, which led to being booted out of their home. Then, luck struck when my boyfriend Christopher Zulu from Ntcheu, who then worked at Malawi Housing Corporation in Blantyre, came to Lilongwe and took me to Blantyre. When I wrote a letter updating my father about my whereabouts he instructed me to send back the chitenje (fabric wrap around) that my mum had given me. As I wrapped and sent back the chitenje, I failed to figure out how else I could regain my father's favour. My apology carried no weight- it only widened the gap between me and my father. A few months later we were blessed with our first-born daughter, Bertha in 1980 followed by a son, Patrick in 1982.

My ambition to be employed set me to apply and interview at Malawi Broadcasting Corporation, Malawi Revenue Authority (MRA) and then secure a job at Lever Brothers. It was a blessing in disguise when my husband left Blantyre upon securing employment with a construction company. I resigned to follow him although I hated that I became a housewife again. A few months later I applied and went to St Anne's' Midwifery School in Nkhotakota. Little did I know that my husband silently applied for me to undergo training as a teacher which I had earlier refused. I complied, quit nursing and went to Lilongwe Teachers' College. That same year I received a letter of success to start work at Malawi Broadcasting Corporation as an announcer. This was based on interviews done two years prior. I was in a hurry, decided to dump my husband's choice, but he put me in a fix.

"If you don't want to be a teacher, come back to take care of the family."

I shed tears at the lost opportunity. Upon graduating as a teacher, we arranged to formalize our marriage in Dedza. My father was pleased to hear that I had become a teacher. Hence, I taught standard two then later requested to teach the next higher class every year. After I taught standard eight I requested the teaching authorities to post me to a correspondence Secondary School. It worked and I smiled as I commenced teaching at St. Kizito Distance Education Centre. That same year I applied, succeeded and underwent a Diploma study at Domasi Teachers' College in Zomba.

Back home one day a neighbor, a woman whispered to me, "These women laugh at you. They claim your husband now does your female roles. One day he will remarry."

Even my mother-in-law lamented, "Why leave my son and these children?" I did not answer back, but I was unstoppable. My husband advised me to ignore them.

I encouraged one woman who accepted, went back to a night secondary school and passed. She too went to a teacher college. Unfortunately, her husband died just after she completed her course and after the funeral the gossipers envied her that she would ably take care of her family singlehandedly.

Upon graduation I was posted to teach at Chichiri Secondary School, so for four years I taught Form one, then two, three and four. While I wondered what my next line of achievement would be, in 1999 I heard a radio advert for producers and presenters at Malawi Broadcasting Corporation (MBC). I immediately forwarded an application, was interviewed and was hired. One of my brainchild programmes was 'Mai Wamakono' (A Woman of Today). I was inspired by break-throughs that some outstanding women had made. Among the notable women interviewed were former president of Malawi, Mrs. Joyce Banda who by then chaired National Association of Business Women in Malawi (NABW), and Mrs. Anastazia Msosa who was then a high court judge.

In 2001, MBC management trained in development journalism then seconded to the Development Broadcasting Unit of MBC. Our Kenyan manager sponsored me in driving, and the first car I drove for three years was a Land Rover. I visited my father with the Land Rover; we found him drinking chibuku, local beer made from fermented maize.

I felt pride and joy as he crowned me saying, "Now you are the pillar of our family."

In 2003 I got a scholarship through the Joint OXFAM Programme in Malawi, and earned a post graduate certificate in Non Governmental Organisations' Management with Imperial College, University of London. I passed with a credit and I was very glad that long at last I had regained closeness to my parents. In 2005 I applied and got a scholarship from National Media Institute, went to the Rhodes University in South Africa to study Media Leadership and Management with the Sol Plaatje Media Institute. My face was awash with smiles on this long awaited first flight, the fantastic scenery of Tambo International Airport, Johannesburg town then to Graham's town, home to Rhodes University.

One day I met an old European woman near the university library. She had a walking stick to support her balance. We greeted, and she told me of her pride as she was doing her master's in education after she had retired long ago.

When I told her that I failed to make it to university she looked at me, held my hand and said, "Look at me. I just turned 60 years old. I will not die before I attain my first degree. Go back to school."

I was 48 years old while I met this woman and thought she was my angel. I promised to take the next action.

With my husband we bought a plot at Machinjiri Area 12, after which we purchased four more plots. We now have planted over fifty fruit trees, another long time dream realised.

Another milestone was that I applied and studied Community Development at the Malawi Polytechnic and passed with higher credit. In 2008 I applied for, interviewed with and then joined Story Workshop Educational Trust (SWET), a local media organization. I then applied to a private university which was accredited by the Malawi Government-Blantyre International University and continued studying community development. I then joined a class level which our fourth born daughter Caroline Zulu was in. I did distant learning while I continued doing community work.

As we chatted, my husband commented that my teaching career had developed me and I thanked him. Sadly, he passed on in 2013 before I graduated in 2014.

I marveled as Professor Charles Chamthunya encouraged me, "Congratulations. Always aim high."

I smiled while inwardly recalling, "Aim high, never tire."

My continued search for career advancement resurfaced when in 2017 I applied, selected and started a Master of Health and Behavior Change Communication at the Malawi Polytechnic University. Out of 38 students who started, only 16 remain. The rest gave up, but I am determined to score.

I discovered my writing potential upon being tasked to write community stories for projects' visibility. One of the feature articles I wrote was "Kanthu nkhama motomoto" (hard work pays). Mr. Sambalikagwa Mvona, an editor of the magazine Moni (Greetings) selected this article and invited me to join the Malawi Writers' Union.

Since then, I am always close to my pen and paper. One of my writings is Flight to Success, an inspirational article, that was published in the Bachelor of Chikanda, an anthology of the Malawi Writers' Union. Through continued personal efforts I have undergone international training by FEMRITE Uganda Women Writers, an all Women Writers' Workshop in Kampala, Uganda, in 2011. While there I interacted and contributed to an African Women Writers' Anthology, Summoning the Rains, in 2012 with my short story, Knife Pleat Skirt. The story was derived from a gender-based violence incident which is believed to have occurred in a Malawian community. I was further privileged when I got a scholarship to join active female writers from some African countries at Rockefeller Foundation, Bellagio Centre in Milan, Italy. There we setup the African Women Writer's Network.

Bear with me, that not all goals will be achieved, not every dream will come true but you must stay in motion while you stay focused. Surmount any discomfort on your life journey for I have never seen a storm last forever. Don't ever give up. Rise up soon after every fall because your best stories will come from your struggles. I am unique because I always turn my failures into seeds for my next achievement.

Life Can Change

Sarai Changalusa Chimombo

Sarai Changalusa Chimombo was born in 1989 and was the first born in a family of three. She graduated from the University of Malawi The Polytechnic in 2011 with a Bachelor of Science in Environmental Health. She is a practicing Occupation Health and Safety specialist and currently the Health, Safety, Security and Environmental Manager for government owned National Oil Company of Malawi.

Sarai is married with one daughter. She lives in Lilongwe and enjoys reading, writing and singing.

Losing parents is definitely the greatest tragedy that can befall any child. It was a cold sunny day and although mother had been sick for a while it was always lovely to see her smiling face every morning before I went to play. She enjoyed having us too and playing with my baby sister. She didn't have much strength but had the love that made us all smile. She was sick but she was around for us to see.

When I saw the car drive in and carry her off that morning, my heart skipped. The way they carried her, it was like she was lifeless. And true to my fears, that was the last I saw of her. I didn't cry like the older women did when we went to church for her service that afternoon. I didn't wail like my aunts and others did when they threw sand over her at the grave. But I cried that night when we went home and she wasn't in her room anymore. I cried the next morning when I didn't see her and saw how tiny my little sister was. At least I will remember the way mother talked and smiled, my sister did not have the chance to build memories with mother.

She left three of us that day, my little brother and sister and me as the big girl. I was only ten years old. All of our property was grabbed by bad family members and there was no inheritance for us. We moved from home to home because we didn't have our own. We were eventually separated so our new guardians could adequately manage. It was my little brother who moved out to another home. We grew apart and our relationship grew cold for we didn't have the time to spend together to bond as siblings. The guilt of all this weighed heavily on me. I felt I should do something as the older one. They looked up to me.

I walked to school every day, always late, always the one to get chastised by the teachers. They didn't know I had chores to do before I report for class every morning, taking care of three babies and running house chores.

When I went for holidays, everyone felt pity. They collected old clothes that I would take the day I went back. I envied the new clothes that my friends had. And when I went to boarding school, their parents came most weekends and brought so many fancy new clothes and good food.

I knew I had to do something, to find a way out. I thought about my siblings every day in school and spent most break times crying in corners. Life couldn't be this way forever. My siblings deserved better. At least they should have some of the things I didn't have.

School was the only hope for me. I knew if I worked hard enough, I would get a good job. I wanted to be a lawyer so I could make a lot of money and help my siblings. So, when I wrote my Primary School Leaving Certificate Exams that year, I prayed "God please let me be selected to secondary school." Because I was told that if I failed I would sit at home and be the nanny, so I worked hard and prayed hard. When the results came, I made it. I was going to secondary school.

Life can be hard when you are a teenager and you don't have the fancy things that others have. Boys don't fancy you because you look shabby and there are some who take advantage of your situation. One day an old man tried to seduce me with a K500.00 note. He was a family friend. I threw his money and ran away. You cannot afford to lose your future for temporal pleasure. Mother was a strong Christian and she taught me values. It was that faith which gave me self-discipline and self-control. I stayed away from the boys.

Sometimes the heaviest of loads are lifted when you find someone to confide in. When you lose a parent, you lose a confidant. Most orphans die in silence because it's not easy to find someone you trust to share your deepest fears with. I found a mentor in my home economics teacher at secondary school. She was a graduate from Chancellor College and she inspired me. I talked to her a lot and she encouraged me. Seeing her everyday walk down the corridors of the school was motivation enough. I had to be like her. She told me about college and I knew I had to go there, so I worked my way through secondary school and wrote my final exams. They were the determining factor now. If I passed and went to college, my whole dream would be fulfilled. But, if I failed, I would be back at home because private colleges were expensive and I couldn't afford them.

It is true that hard work pays, and even though the road may not lead straight to where you want, positive efforts get you closer. I passed with flying colors and was selected to go to college. Many people get too excited in college, lose focus and are eventually expelled. It's good to be focused and surround yourself with the right friends in order to make it. Even though I never became a lawyer, I eventually graduated with a Bachelor's in Environmental Health. It was not long before I got my first job and I quickly rose through the ladder to become a manager at a young age.

I eventually found the right man and we got married two years after college. Today we have a daughter whom we are shaping to become more that what I have become. I am able to support my siblings and others too. I finally have a home, my home.

There are countless times I still feel the pain of orphan hood. Like the day I graduated from college, I wished mother was there to give me flowers and the day I walked down the aisle and someone else stood in for father. The pain doesn't completely go away.

I have learnt over time that losing parents is not the worst tragedy, it's when you let yourself sink into grief and lose focus. The destiny of each of us is inside and when you are focused, you can turn your life around to become better than your past. When you lose the ones you love, don't lose yourself because when the sun sets every day, it rises again more beautiful the next morning. That's how life can change.

The Woman Power

Sumeya Issa

Sumeya Issa is a 21 year old young Malawian female who is currently pursuing a bachelor's degree in journalism at the Malawi Polytechnic. Miss Issa hopes to further pursue her studies in a different country once she attains her first degree. She believes exposure and knowledge are essential for every human being who seeks to impact the world.

She is passionate about poetry and written works, where she spends most of her time writing (mainly poetry) and exploring works from different artists she sources her inspirations from. She equally believes that while journalism remains an undermined profession in some parts of the world, it is the one discipline that has liberated many people from silence.

"The joy is in breaking the silence & ensuring that the minority have a voice."

"You have a superpower," she would say to me. There was so much light in my mother's eyes every time she uttered those words. I was eighteen when I realized what she meant, that all women have a superpower. I have a superpower. I am different. I am capable. I am many things, but a failure.

I still have distant memories of my father. I have spoken to him before, in my lonely and devastated moments, and I have shared with him my greatest fears, my dreams. I sometimes tell father how I really need to make mum proud of me one day. I was only four when he died, although somehow, I have always felt his presence - like he never left - but he did, and that's the kind of pain I will never be able to erase. It is pain from within. Giving up is what most women do, especially after their support system dies, in this case my father. Women give up, but my mother didn't. My mother fought, she fought until she was certain we would be okay again, all three of us. Her, my elder brother and me.

Mother told me school was important. I felt like she only started to emphasize this many years after father's death, like it was the only thing left to live for. If I am honest, I hated every conversation about school. My friends had their fathers to boast about, so I created a lie, that my father was alive somewhere in a foreign land. It was the only way to fit in and avoid the many questions that I had no clear answers to. The truth is, even I had many questions about father's death, so I learnt how to pray. I would pray until I felt okay again. I never told mum that I hated school, and as painful as it was, I pulled myself out of bed every morning to go, including the cold mornings of June. To encourage my brother and I, mother would buy small presents for us when we did extremely well in school. I remember one time getting new shoes when I passed my exams with good grades and from that time I was motivated to go on. I studied more, worked harder and slowly started to discover my passion for writing.

If I tell this story, and my mother is not apart of it, then it is incomplete. Mothers are pillars they say, well mine is my light. My fight for education as a colored woman begun when I was eighteen. I had always been different, race being one of the major contributing factors and there weren't many girls like me pursuing higher education. At eighteen, I was on a whole new journey to defeat my fears and dislikes. I had decided that no matter what happened and no matter how society perceived me that I would graduate from college and inspire other young women. In 2014, I started my journey as a student journalist at the University of Malawi Polytechnic. I am a product of one of the top Catholic secondary schools in the country. We had girls that attained scholarships to America for being top of the class at MSCE (Malawi School Certificate of Education) level. How I got into boarding school is a whole new chapter, but there is where I learnt how to dream.

I have been asked what I am still doing in college, and it is often times because of the color of my skin. I have been reminded by the same world that claims to embrace diversity that girls like me belong in the kitchen. And as much as this perception is not very far from reality, I have not embraced it as my truth. I have decided to embrace my superpower instead. When mother would tell me about superpowers, she meant the men that

I would one day meet, the ones who would try to rob me of my dreams. She told me that only I have the power to decide what my tomorrow will look like. Mother meant there would be times that she would struggle to pay my college tuition, and that when I cannot sense my woman power, that only God would be able to regenerate it. Mother meant that there would be trouble, but that we are not ever to give up.

In my twenty one years of living, I have come to the realization that the world is a tough place for any woman to survive. With time, we create our own walls and those walls are a way to protect ourselves. I have been motivated by my desire to be different, my desire to one day impact the world with the knowledge I have attained through education. There were times I could have chosen to drop out of school, to find an easy way out, but the secret I discovered is that there is no easy way out.

Education provides women with the ultimate tool that no man can destroy. It is knowledge that we will carry to the grave . It's a power we must embrace. Knowing this, I chose to be the colored woman who did not opt for marriage at a tender age. I choose to communicate the power of other fellow women to the outside world. I choose to use my education as a tool to encourage and motivate other females both young and old.

In April 2017, mother came home from work one blissful evening with a newspaper in her hand. Smiling and excited, she flipped through the pages and placed her fingers on one particular section. "You should apply," she said. I was a little intimidated with the confidence in her voice but lifted the page from her hand instead. "What is it, mum?" I asked.

"They are looking for young journalists from all over the world who can attend a workshop in the UK. It is only for a few days but you should try applying!" I was not confident in the beginning, but gave it a try anyway. A few months later, I received an email from the British Council telling me that I had been selected for the workshop in Edinburgh, Scotland. I had never felt so fulfilled in my entire life. The feeling that raced within me is still indescribable.

This opportunity allowed me to represent my country in a foreign land. I was one of 98 applicants selected to represent their countries in Edinburgh. Malawi had two representatives, both my friend and I. It was a life changing experience that I was able to take on because I am still at school, studying journalism which is exactly what this short-term scholarship required. Had I chosen to embrace the perceptions of people and focused more on how I look rather than what I am capable of, I would have never gotten that scholarship. I consider this one of my greatest successes in life and I am yet to achieve more.

As a writer and aspiring journalist, I would like to use my voice to promote equality among all races. I want to help women to speak out their fears, hopes and dreams. I would like both my intellectual and motivational work to remind the youth that they are the future. My career path creates room for individuals from all walks of life, where the illiterate who cannot read or write will watch and listen and where the blind cannot see they will listen and feel. Education is what every girl needs to unveil her superpower. I would like to thank my Mother, Fortina for leading me to that truth.

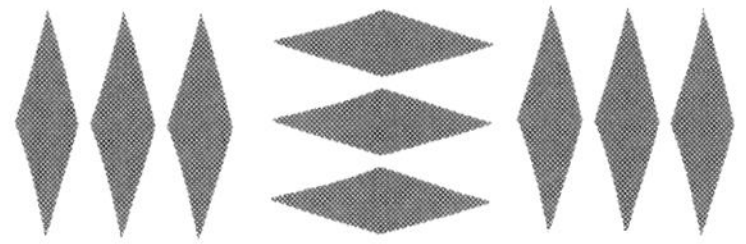

My Stepfather's Love Molded Me Into The Woman I Am

Susan Diss Phiri

Susan is a graduate of the University of Malawi with a diploma in Agriculture (Diplomas in Malawi are a Pre-baccalaureate level much like a junior college diploma). In her family she was the first born of seven. She was abandoned by her father who never took responsibility and then was raised by her mother and her stepfather.

Susan's hardships are unimaginable to most people outside of Africa, yet she overcame them one at a time and still continues to do so. Currently she coordinates projects for various Non-Government Organizations (NGOs). She is also the author of a series of articles published in Malawi reflecting on the story of her life and how she derives her strength from all the things she had to overcome. She also gives back by working for a Christian missionary organization.

Here is her story in her own words.

In the Beginning

Once upon a time, four decades ago there was a woman, my mother, who was impregnated by a man who did not accept his responsibility for bringing me into the world. My mother had no formal education, had lost her father while she was very young yet took charge for bringing me into the world. I was born underweight, probably through nutritional deficiencies. Later, my mother married an uneducated but good man who sold dry fish to earn his living. Although lacking in education, he had a dream that I would get the education he did not get and achieve the dreams he could not.

My stepfather worked very hard to support a family of eight kids yet never complained about the poor quality of his life. Instead, he stressed his love for me and the other kids he fathered.

I made it through primary school with flying colors and was selected to enroll in one of the best girls' secondary schools in Malawi. Although I had very limited resources, I was able to go to Bunda College of Agriculture, part of the University of Malawi and my stepfather worked hard to pay the fees.

Unfortunately for me and my family my loving stepfather who was chronically ill a great deal of his life passed away during my first year in college leaving behind my mother and seven children, six of whom he fathered, and me who he gave all the love possible. To me, he was my true dad. "Diss" was his family name and "Phiri" was my mother's. I have never used the last name of the man who impregnated my mother. My stepfather was really my dad.

Bad Winds Blow in my Face While in College

By the time I was in my second year of college life was very tough for me. I had to pay the required contribution fee to stay in college yet I had no money. I had to beg for paper to take notes in class and my younger siblings were selling vegetables to earn money instead of going to school. I was ashamed that I did not have the money to buy paper to take notes in college and my lack of concentration was tearing me apart. I would spend nights weeping and awaken with swollen, red eyes. It was not the right thing to continue my college career. Pure and simple I did not have the resources to do so.

Instead, I decided to push through and be thankful for obtaining my two year diploma in agriculture and forego my desire to complete the full degree program. Once I finished the diploma program, I began to take care of my mother and my six siblings. By that time my two brothers had gone into early marriages, but the other four kids were either doing drugs or wandering aimlessly. My youngest brother was not even 10 years old.

Then, to further complicate my life, all of a sudden, my mother fell ill and died leaving me as the head of the family with no choice but to take care of the rest of the clan. By then, my youngest brother had turned 10 years old. My goal became to have all of my unmarried siblings under one roof, love them all, and put aside my ambition to help them become independent, good citizens.

In the End a Better Life Looked Me in the Eyes

I prayed and worked hard, and then I prayed some more and about a year later I became a District Civil Education Officer. I had four siblings under my roof and felt like a million dollars. Now in my early 40's I plan to finish my bachelor's degree. I aim to complete my education however my life also includes helping the needy. Looking at how my siblings almost moved to live on the streets, I brought into my home two teenagers and helped them get their high school education. Where my life will take me I do not know, however, I have to do what is right, and pray I don't make mistakes. To other girls in Malawi and other parts of Africa I offer the following suggestions:

First, make use of the resources you have to attain the best education you can. Push on and never give up. Give a smile to others even though you have little, for in the long run your education will pave a way to achieve a better livelihood.

Second, to step mothers and fathers. Love your step child as your own, as this will open a child's heart and encourage him or her to work to achieve a better life. I still love and remember my step dad, although he is long dead and only lived a short life, he gave me a reason to smile and looks after me from the other side.

Third, be thankful for what you have and keep your family close to your heart. Don't underestimate the power of a family that is together. You can move mountains if your entire family is with you.

Strive for honesty. If we want to combat corruption, we must embrace honesty. If being honest drives some of your friends away, stay honest and give up your friends, as they are not truly your friends. Honesty will give you peace inside, and without honesty, our nations collapse into a maelstrom of corruption.

Finally, be proud and thank God for what you have received and thank yourself for what you have done with the resources you had.

Yes, I will get there. I have a job, and a good family and I will complete my education. It has not been easy but I have turned lemons into excellent lemonade. Never lose hope. Stay the course. Stay strong.

The Audacity to Turn Wrong Into Right

Yacinta Phiri

"You can dream all you want, but if you don't take action nothing will happen" is her favourite line. Yacinta Phiri is a 25 year old woman who is currently the Vice President of the Lilongwe chapter of the Loving Arms Christian organisation. She holds a bachelor's degree in agriculture and applied economics from the Lilongwe University of Agriculture and Natural Resources (LUANAR).

Yacinta has passion for female empowerment and would like to see more women and girls participate in economic activities to aid the growth of the country. She wants to pursue entrepreneurship in real estate business and believes that prayer, hard work, determination and perseverance drives one to achieve their goals and, believes that for change to come one must start by changing themselves. In her free time Yacinta likes to read books, volunteering for charity organisations and dancing to keep herself fit.

One afternoon around five o'clock in the evening, I sat down on our veranda and one by one the students from Bunda College of Agriculture and Natural resources passed by going to the boy's quarters where they resided. One of the questions which lingered in my mind was "What does it take to be selected here?" In my mind these students were the most intelligent students I had ever seen. I would hear people say that it was hard to finish at Bunda, that either you would have to repeat or be withdrawn. Only a few would finish and get their degree. This made me automatically stop myself from pursuing any programs being offered at this school.

My mind raced back to my former secondary school, where I was considered a troublesome girl. I had no idea why I was going to school, no written goals nor any idea what I would study in college. Every morning during assembly my name would not be missed when called. From form one to form four I lived the life of a lost child who had no direction. During my form three I was suspended twice for violence as well as disobedience. A month before our final MANEB exams and after the results came out I had 37 points, all of which I deserved. Regrets piled up and as I sat on that veranda that evening I thought to myself, I am a failure!

The veranda became my reflection space, I would usually sit there with the nine month old baby of my sister who had married a lecturer. She was usually not home as her work required her to go in the field, so the baby would stay with me and his older brother who was three years old. I pretty much had a tough job. I would play with these children almost every evening just to pass time and to make the baby sleep. It was going towards the end of the year and I had stayed home almost a year without doing anything except helping my sister raise her kids.

One afternoon I decided to clean up the room and I came across a book called "Gifted Hands," by Dr. Ben Carson. Yes, I was a troublesome child but I never lost the hunger to read novels because that was what I used to spend my time on. But this was a very different story, not the mills and boons we knew back in secondary school. This was a biography, the life of someone called Ben Carson, once a failure who became the youngest director of pediatric neuro-surgery in the United States of America. I thought to myself that I could relate and I told myself that I can try reading this type of book.

One evening after reading half of the book, I told my sister that I wanted to change my life and how I look at things. I told her about the book and how it was changing my life. My sister was very supportive and told me that if she saw a change in me that she would pay my school fees at the school of my choice. She also told me that helping her take care of the children contributed to this decision. At first caring for them was a burden, but spending so much time on the veranda had made me to start thinking about my life. I realized that sometimes things are given to us to teach us lessons and find ourselves. What we consider burdens might be a stepping stone to search for and find ourselves.

In 2010 when school opened for the second term, I found myself in a new secondary school. I was determined, had written down goals and was certain that I would not come out of that school empty handed. I said goodbye to my biological mother who had come with me. As usual I was fighting back the tears and the pain that were on my chest . I met my new head master and he made one statement which never leaves my mind, "If you do not understand mathematics from me, you will never understand it anywhere." Haha! What a threat but maybe that is what I wanted to hear.

I worked hard, and met a girl who became my best friend in the entire school. I had no one but her because like me, she came to repeat her courses and together we started form three. We were called "wobweleza" which meant "those who repeated the classes". It didn't bother us because this time we had come with a goal. If you have a goal and are determined to achieve it, you become deaf to the voices which want to disturb you. With the help of my friend and determined headmaster and teachers, my failure became history. I remember I hated Physical Science and Mathematics, but this time around they became my best friends. Time had traveled so fast and it was already time to write my final exams. Wow! I did not even notice. In 2011 I sat for the final exams and went home peacefully. During the holiday, I wrote in my diary that I would pass with 15-19 points and that I wanted to pursue Agriculture Economics at Bunda.

I am a Catholic by faith and had a 9 day prayer called a novena. One afternoon as I was going to the market with my mother I received a message that our entrance exams were out. I waited till I got home to learn my fate and had never felt so anxious. My stomach went rumbling and I went to use the toilet more than three times. I had never experienced these things in my first attempt. When you want it so badly you are eager to know the results so you become anxious and worry a lot.

"More than two hundred students have been withdrawn from this school," said the Dean of students on the day we were being oriented. I was taken back to those rumors from a long time ago, but this did not scare me at all. I told myself that I made it this far so I can make it to the fourth year and get my degree. Agriculture and Applied Economics is one of the mathematical programs and I wouldn't have made it this far if

I had not made mathematics my best friend. This taught me that we fail because we do not try enough.

The journey continued until I finished, without repeating any classes. I remember during my third year, my supervisor resigned. This was a great shock to me because it meant that I had to change supervisors and change my project to suit his style. Situations can change but what matters is how strongly you believe in yourself and the work that you do.

Eight years down the line, I had 19 points and graduated on the 21st of March 2018 with a Bachelor's of Science in Agriculture and Applied Economics. I believe that if what I have achieved and what I'm going to do is in God's willing, I will.

It's not a matter of competing with others or who is doing better than me. It's not about who is praying the right way. It's about the faith, belief, determination, hard work, patience and the relationship that you have with God. You can achieve anything, whether you want to be an actress, pastor or musician. Whatever gift you have, comes from God. Your goals determine what drives you. Find a mentor. Ben Carson was my mentor through his book, and my sister in person. I still have a goal to become a successful female entrepreneur in the Malawi real estate business. I still believe that if God continues giving me the gift of life then everything is possible.

THE POEMS

The poets and storytellers in the second section of the anthology are the sounds of the future, the sweet music of young girls believing in their bright minds and ability to create positive change. Given an education, they can grow beyond what even they can imagine. Their thundering cries for knowledge can be heard in the rhythm of their crisp, newfound voices.

Voices for Change camp leaders Chikondi Lunguzi Njawala and Lisa Borden are certified facilitators in the AWA creative writing method. In a welcoming space of non-judgment, Chikondi and Lisa offered the girls an opportunity to explore their writing voices.

A clear, simple prompt was provided to spark memory or imagination. A simple sentence stem such as, "Begin writing with the words, "I feel strong when…," is one example of a prompt. Following a ten to twenty minute free writing period participants were invited to read if they chose to, receiving positive feedback on their writing. Following a lesson in editing with Heather Borden, camp assistant, the girls submitted their pieces for publication. Imagine their delight and increased confidence when they see their words in print for the first time!

VoiceFlame is especially proud of our two thriving college students, authors and poets, Mphatso Major and Gladys James, who attend the University of Malawi, Polytechnic and Lilongwe University of Agriculture and Natural Resources, respectfully. Under the nurturing guidance of Chikondi and Lisa, Gladys and Mphatso have matured from tight buds afraid to display their brilliance into the unrestrained lavender blossoms of the Jacaranda tree.

I hope you enjoy reading these written works as much as I have appreciated being a part of bringing it together. Like the unforgettable splendor of a fiery African sunset, these stories and poems remain permanently etched into my heart. Together, may we all – parents, teachers, political leaders, sons and daughters - awaken to the necessity and urgency of educating girls everywhere.

Mary Tuchscherer
Executive Director, VoiceFlame

Our Mother VoiceFlame

Gladys James

It was a heavy flame
burning inside a hungry woman's heart
a thirst having no foresight to get ended

Heavy heart holding heavy silence
but no one was willing to end the silence
Women and girls scared to die
without their voices being heard

VoiceFlame came in
wondered how hard the silence was like on the ground
Voice out through the
Amherst Writers and Artists (AWA)
becomes a solution

Encouraging women and girls to go back to school
completely kill the silence
now women are heard

It was like a phone call
calling all girls to go back to school
to sharpen their writing skills

Now VoiceFlame has become our mother
a mother who hears our cries
and able to wash away the flooding rivers on our faces
A mother who knows how to care for her children
A mother hoping for a bright future
A mother who always be there fighting for our rights

What a lovely mother are you dear?
You bring happiness and hope to your kids
you know what is best for us
see how your kids have grown up

Girls, the ball, it is in our hands now
Let us hold our hands tightly
let's unite, where we will be bonded together,
no one to break us apart
don't be afraid
because we are together
with a caring mother

VoiceFlame

Never Look Back

Alinafe Zamaele

My friends, never look back
be focused on what you're doing
know you are beautiful, girls
but some people will try to destroy your future

My friends, never look back
this world is full of cheaters
cheaters who will cheat girls
be ready
so that what comes around
does not beat the drum

My friends, never look back
I know that you have a chance
to go to college
to get a good job
please, please
ever forward, not backward!

My friends, never look back
the good things of this world
will not run from you
you will find them
when you finish school
your future is ahead
look forward, not back
at where you're coming from

Wake Up, Girls!

Alinafe Zamaele

Wake up, wake up, girls
open your eyes and see
where the world is going

Wake up, wake up, girls
we can change the world
through our unique voices

Wake up, wake up, girls
we can do great things
that people say only boys can do
we are favoured, girls
we have unique voices

Wake up, wake up, girls
arise and shine in the world
like the moon in the sky
a light in the darkness
helping people know
that we are special

The Hidden Truth

Annabel Munyenyembe

I don't know what it is
The sadness of women always
Underestimating themselves
Thinking they can't do anything
Always sharing the sorrow, shame and heartaches
And not the beautiful ideas for change

Let's talk about the housewives
I hear them cry
We better make a change
Let's all bring the encouraging world to friends
We can make a difference

Arise girls
Arise women
Have we been brainwashed?
Or is it that we don't know?
We don't know what we carry on our shoulders
You amaze me
Understanding ourselves can't bring change

Awake! Awake!
The hidden truth is here

Girls like us bring the future change

No educated girls?
No new voices?

The next generation will suffer
The next generation will cry
They will get married early
Their children will starve
They will die young

Nothing is good here

We better make a change

What Strengthens Me

Annabel Munyenyembe

I normally feel strong when I pray and eat first thing in the morning. It was 6:30am and I was still asleep in bed. My brother knocked on my door. "Annabel! Annabel!" I couldn't hear. I was so tired from the previous day that I hadn't heard my alarm clock. He continued knocking. I finally woke up and it was 6:45am. I was, like, "Oh my gosh!!! I have an exam at 8am and it take me more than an hour to get to school!" I thought about how long it takes to get ready every morning. I usually take an hour and a half getting ready before I head off to school. I felt nervous now because I knew that if I took this long for preparation, I would definitely be late for my exam.

This exam paper was the one that would determine whether or not I can go to university! I spent about 5 minutes thinking about what I should do and then it was already 6:50! I had to rush. I didn't eat. I just brushed my teeth sprayed so much perfume on myself! Then I starting running to catch a bus.

When I reached the bus stand, the queue was just too long. I thought maybe I should forget the bus and get a bicycle taxi. Just as I stepped out of the bus queue, my teacher, the one who would be giving me the exam, saw me. She stopped her car, called me over and gave me a lift. I felt so relieved because I knew I wouldn't be late for this exam after all. We got there with just 10 minutes to go before the beginning of the exam paper and I had time to relax a little bit. To my surprise, it was the simplest paper ever!

My Future

Beatrice Mbengwani

I can see my future being bright
I'll be a self-dependent woman
I see success in myself
Yes, I see myself
Working in media
All this because
I have access to education

I can see my future
Achieving in many areas
Playing many roles
I know I will be whoever I want to be
I don't want to work for someone else
Someone should work for me
For real
I want to be independent

I can see a light shining on my future
This light is education
I don't want to be like some women
Who ask for money from their husbands to buy their undies
They don't have their own money
because they depend on their husbands
I know that I will achieve my goals

I Hold a Key

Beatrice Mbengwani

I hold a key
A key of destination
Not destruction
Yes to the nation
Beneficial to the coming generation
Yes, as a media worker at my station
Bringing to an end the issue of violation
Yes, the violation of girls' rights in our nation

I hold a key
A key to my success and happiness
But only if I have the access
Yes the access to education, but only if I improve my kindness
And handle properly my weakness
Loving others, not being merciless or heartless
I know I will be a witness
Ooohhh, yes, a witness to my own success

I hold a key
A key which opens the bright future
I will be against our culture
Which affects the bright future
Yes, the future of young girls and destruction of their treasure
And end up with the Malawians' nature
The nature of taking away one's pasture
This pasture refers to their bright future
Forcing early marriage as their culture

I hold a key

When Women Are Together

Elizabeth Mpaweni

When women are together
oh, yes! they say to each other
hard work is like open handbags
that are full of money
they help each other with good hair styles
and put on expensive makeup
they look beautiful
When women are together
each one is proud
of her husband
where he works - how he loves her
what he does for her birthday
they are women of love
kindness and faith
When women are together
they ask each other questions
like what colour do they like most
because likes and dislikes are different
knowing these things about your friends
is a way to respect them
they are careful with these differences
to avoid disappointment and disagreements
When women are together
they share their beliefs with one another
though they have different churches
they have fun together
and have one decision in common
this shows that God is
real and at work
every day, every hour,
he is faithful

How Can We Progress?

Elizabeth Mpaweni

How can we progress?
God's plan for us is good
plans to prosper
to praise Him without pain
I like, I love this
almighty Father of all people
I thank you for everyone
How can we progress?
Working hard with all our hearts to break poverty
it is not our portion
don't be lazy
rise up by your fingers
stand up for your rights
How can we progress?
Always be focused
respect what others say
a writer respects others
by listening to them
How? Attentively, with purpose
as they tell a story
because everyone's voice is unique
How can we progress?
Time is money
always keep time
use a watch
follow priorities in the right order
don't punish yourself
set the priorities you want for your life
early in the morning
and the day will be sweet
and smell like chocolate

Like a Dream

Elvance Mseteka

Oh, like a dream that is true
you change everything in my life
you make me an honourable person
like our president

Like a dream
you make me speak
like an American
You help me make a decision
that I won't leave you till death
because when I was young
I didn't believe
my voice is unique

Like a dream
yes, I'm still saying like a dream
because you help me to read and write
You let me know so many people
like Lisa and her daughter
I know you have love for me
and for my future because you are
VoiceFlame

Who Are You?

Elvance Mseteka

Who are you?
My question is
Who are you?
you have no relative
friends or neighbours
Who are you?
Oh, dear, I'm still asking
so many questions
about you
I've heard so many stories
that people say about you
Who are you?
Some people say
if a person wants to find you
she needs to read and write so many things
using her voice
Who are you?
Are you a person
or an animal?
Maybe you are a bird
that can fly away
I'm not sure
Who are you?
I've also heard it said
that if someone wants to achieve her goals
she needs to listen to her teacher carefully
when she is speaking
The examination could be based
on words coming from her mouth

Who are you?

In my mind
I will give you a name
From today
you are education

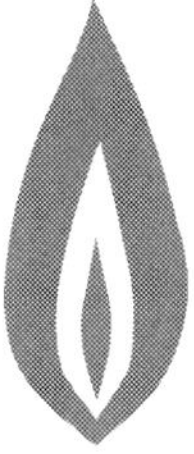

You Sleep Like Whom?

Elvance Mseteka

When I'm sleeping
I sleep like a queen
because a queen's voice is unique
She speaks about this and that
she dreams that one day
she will rule the whole world

When I'm sleeping
I sleep like a hare
because when a hare sleeps
it sleeps without closing its eyes
so I can improve my country
For if a thief comes
he will never steal my future
because I am alert

When I'm sleeping
I sleep like the president's soldier
because she sleeps while standing
she is ready for any attack
likewise I can be prepared
for any challenges
using my education as my solution

Now it's over to you my friends
You sleep like whom?
Answer me carefully
my question will help you
and make you special

I Hold a Key

Esther Kajawo

I hold a key
which will open the thinking capacity
in my mind
and my mind will change the world

I hold a key
It is as silver as a silver lining
It is little in size
but it protects me and my family
It has a hole in the middle of it
Oh! I can see a lick in my future
so I need a key to open my future
and the key is education

I Am On Fire

Esther Kajawo

I am on fire
Yes I am on fire
to be a judge
to judge many cases
to fulfill my dreams
and the dream of my mother
I work hard and harder
because of what I am on fire for

I am on firc
to have confidence
to finish my dreams
so that I can be a good judge
I want to be above many judges
to be an example to many girls
and an inspiration to many boys

Necklace

Esther Kajawo

My red long necklace, it is so beautiful and it adds beauty to my neck. It has many different colours but I just call it my red necklace because red is my favourite colour. I use it to show off and I believe that those who don't have a beautiful necklace are out of fashion! When I'm in a dark place, my necklace is always bright like a bulb because it is a magical necklace, just like Rapunzele's hair. My necklace is my mystery light.

My New Path

Esther Kajawo

My path in the fourth month was tough
but now my legs are walking on the proper path
because I have learned how to succeed and proceed

I will be active as an activist
protecting all the girls in my country

I will know my rights and do what's right
and will enlighten other people to know their rights

Girls, aspire to be the inspiration
of the nation

I Feel Strong When

Euphemia Mughogho

I feel strong when
I am answering a question in class
I feel strong when
I am writing stories
I feel strong when
I'm in a happy mood
I feel strong when
you are giving feedback
on what I wrote

When Girls are Together

Euphemia Mughogho

When girls are together, they talk about how life goes. They talk about how they can raise their voices up. But there are some girls who always talk about problems. But in this picture of the statue it shows the girls are helping each other solve problems, and sharing ideas on how to achieve their goals in the future.

Women I Admire

Euphemia Mughogho

Julianna Lunguzi
Lovely
Kind
Beautiful
Strong
Powerful

She helps girls and women
to help them achieve their goals

She also helps girls and women
whose rights have been violated

She brings young girls
who are married back to school

She stands as a role model for girls and women

My Future Will Be Different

Euphemia Mughogho

My future will be different
because of the people who encourage me to work hard

My future will be different
because the people I admire, they really work hard

My future will be different
when I focus my life on education and say no to bad behaviour

My future will be different
at the college of Polytechnic

Strong

Euphemia Mughogho

She is strong
she is strong indeed
strong like a lion
she knows she can do it
oh, yes, she can do it
by seeing who she is

She is healthy
she is healthy indeed
she is a woman who is able
to face all the challenges
and solve them

She is feeling strong
as strong as a hippo
this means that as girls
we are strong
and we have the power
to speak up

For All the Girls Who Come After Me

Juliana Banda

All the girls behind me,
all the girls who come after me
walk in a good direction
to be where I am
Chase your dreams as if you are chasing a thief
run away from boys who ruin you
open up your mouth and say no to any dream destroyer
value your body for it more valuable than gold and diamond

All the girls behind me
all the girls who come after me
rise up and be examples to other girls
work hard in class as if you are going to be given salary
refuse to sleep more, like you don't like sleeping.

Refuse to suffer by working hard
don't let your unfinished dream to be shattered
jump high to reach your bright future
aim high to have more confident
use your voice carefully
and let it be your pride
for it is more worthy than silver

When Girls Are Together

Juliana Banda

When girls are together
they chat
they talk about the future
how wonderful women they will be
listening to the one talking carefully
making sure they do not miss anything
they talk about what they want
to become and who they admire
When girls are together
they talk about
what they heard and what they saw
and they also talk about their dressing
the hair style
especially when one has a
new cloth or new shoes
When girls are together
there is a new change
as they are game changers
they encourage each other
that they can make it
just like anyone else
they see wonderful destiny
being somewhere as
it is their biggest passion
When women are together
they dance, they sing
they even help each other with house chores
because hard working is their habit.
they feel free to tell one another
what they are going through
sharing secrets as they know
that is their fellow girls
they show off their new things
just to make the other girl
admire their thing

My Future Will Be Different Because

Juliana Banda

I work hard like my father
I follow my dreams as I am following footsteps
relaxing when I am too tired but not giving up
praying to almighty each and everyday
putting my future in his holy hands
and putting my trust in him.

My future will be different because
I stand on shoulders of those who came before us.
and my future will be different because
I have role models who inspire me
helping me to overcome challenges

I Hold A Key

Juliana Banda

I hold a key
which is a key to my success
this key is called education
It will open
it will not change the world but
it will open minds
and minds will change the world
and a key that will turn me into a leader
a hero and an inspirational to many people

I hold a key
a key that will make
a girl full of possibilities
a key that will remove my fear
and make me to be strong
a key that will help me to speak out
a key to my destiny

I hold a key
The one that can help me to lock the door
meaning that the key to education
will lock every self-esteem and fear
that used to hinder my joy
everything that used to hinder my peace
and I will open good things with this key
as it is a key to success

I Am On Fire

Juliana Banda

I am on fire for my dreams
as a girl
I am on fire for my unfinished dreams
living my dream is what I am on fire for
I do not want my children to suffer
I do not want my relatives to suffer
I want them to see change in their lives

I am on fire for my dreams
I do not want them to be unfulfilled
I don't want to watch them scatter

I am on fire for my dreams.
I wanna be a strong woman
achieving my dreams
achieving my goals, by finishing school
it is my greatest passion
so that one day I may be invited to girls camps to speak
that will make them focus on their dreams

Not Just A Girl

Juliana Banda

I am a girl
But not just a girl
But girl who can do anything just as a man
Not just a girl
But a girl full of possibilities
Full of wonderful goals
A girl who believes in a power of dreams
A strong lady who can make a big change

I am a girl
Not just a girl but a future role model
A great inspiration to many girls
A great future leader even to boys
A hero and a game changer
To many children and women
A girl who can motivate many
A girl of history to many generations

I am not just a girl
But a girl who can heal souls with her voice
I am not just a girl but a girl who can use her voice
To defeat every fear and remove any pain.
I am just a girl, but a strong lady

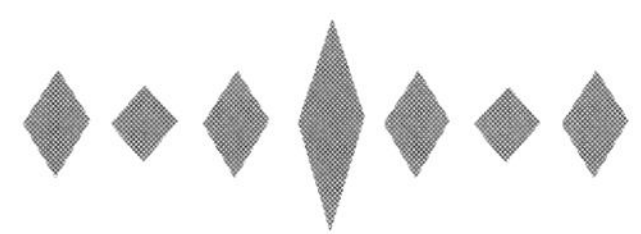

As I Go

Juliana Banda

As I leave here I will go
with a strong and sharp mind
as I have learnt a lot
of things in your beautiful stories and poem

As I leave here I will go
with a lonely heart
but full of encouraging words of yours
full of good ideas
we have been sharing together

As I go I will leave
with sweet memories
because I know I never share
sweet charming words with you again

I know I will miss all of you
Not just you, but your stories,
poems and your amazing quotes

I know that I hold a key
that can open any good door

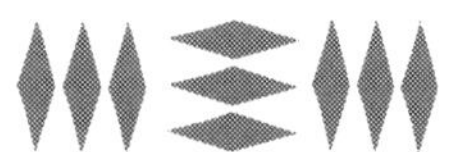

As We Go

Gertrude Tembo

As I leave here
I will remember all the girls
who stayed here together
I will remember every one of us
and I will not forget you, my friends

As I leave here
I will remember the good things that we did together
as one family
I thank you, Lisa and your daughter,
for staying with us
for all the time you spent here

As I leave here
I thank you, Aunt Chiko, and my friends
for showing love
I pray to God to give you a long life

All the best to all of you as we are leaving
because I know that I will meet you again, girls,
another time

Good luck!!

Beautiful Girl

Gertrude Tembo

She is beautiful
more beautiful than anyone
she looks so happy
she is a beautiful girl

I like this girl
she is educated
she is smart and humble
she is a role model
she is a beautiful girl

Everyone admires her
always, she looks so beautiful in
the way she dresses
always, she looks so happy
she is beautiful

I would like to be like her
it's my dream
she is hard working
and perfect
she is a beautiful girl

I Am On Fire

Gertrude Tembo

I am on fire for my education
I have many dreams in my life
I am a hard-working girl

Education is my key
In my dreams I'd like to be a police officer
It's my dream and
I think about it always

I will be a police officer
and will end corruption in my country

I will make sure
that I will achieve what I want
There are some people who say bad things about me
but I won't give up

For All the Girls Who Come After Me

Gladys James

Rise girls, rise

Create a better space in your life
prepare to stand in the strong storm
be able to stand in any circumstance

Open your eyes
and let them focus toward your dreams
never mind the people
who will actually point fingers at you

Move on with your plan
go until you get it
follow your dream
until you get there

Be strong enough
and strength will follow you
Be yourself
and leave the weakness behind you

Keep your voice and believe in it
never get tired of education, instead
let education be the one to get tired of you

Rise girls, rise

As We Go

Gladys James

As I leave here
I now believe
that I am a leader
and my voice
is for change

As I leave here
I will only remain
with the sweet memories
fresh in my mind
all the day

Because I know
and strongly believe
that my mind, my heart and my hands
are the best weapons
to bring change
for it starts with the mind
and then to the heart
before the hands will act
and I will use them as my tools

As I leave here
I will never be afraid
to speak out
for I believe
my voice is unique

As I leave here
I will renew my writing skills
when I go back to school
and I know
I was made with a purpose
a purpose of purpose
in this world

Hear Us Out

Gladys James

"It's in my future, Mum! I have to go back to school! I know my opportunities will open up when I'm given a chance to go on with my education. Look, Mum. I'm still at a tender age and I should be in school. Getting married at this age, it will only kill my dream. I know we are poor, but I strongly believe I can make it. I'm taking your strength and encouragement. Can't you see, Mum?"

The poor and hopeless girl cried into her hands, shocked, as the traditional wedding began. No one thought it was wrong to see her wed in this way. Her voice couldn't be heard. She valued education in her life. She begged her mother to help her out, but her mother had no choice but to let her daughter go. This shouldn't be. Hear us out!

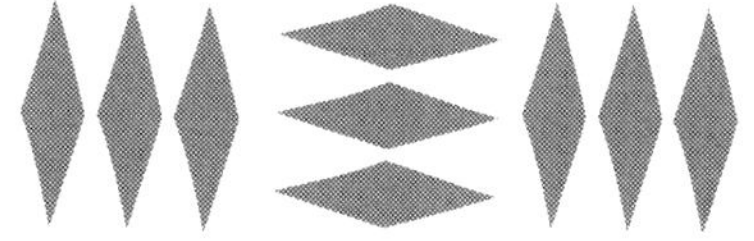

Key

Gladys James

Different keys for different people

I hold a key
a strong and powerful weapon
made of iron

They say education is the key
that will unlock our chances
but why are we stopped
from success in life?

They say the sky is the limit
but why are we denied
some work opportunities
and told we are not meant
to have that kind of work?

They said speak out to be heard
but why don't they
even recognise our voices?

Questions
Without answers

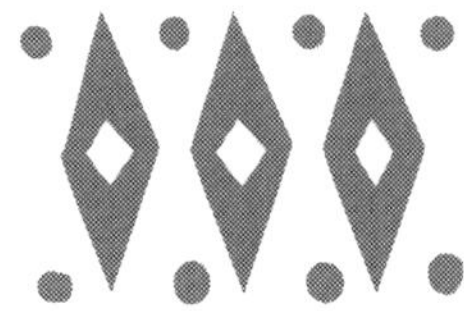

What Am I On Fire For?

Gladys James

I'm on fire for fighting for
what belongs to me
for I believe and have hope

Hope for brighter days
days of joy and focusing on
what is meant to be

No time to waste right now
keep on checking my progress
check every step I'm about to take

Changing the world into a fine
sweet milk and honey world

Pursuing my career
stronger and stronger

I will always be tenacious

Corruption

Gladys James

Corruption
a best friend to the richest
but an enemy of the poor
There they come and go
with big empty bags in their stomach
eating our money
leaving the poor to suffer

They don't even care that
the future generation will suffer
If corruption was a fly I could swallow it
It couldn't survive in the hands of the poor
but it's alive in the hands of the rich

Corruption
a best friend of the people who are in power
you turned them into a lion of hate
the greedy lions who won't even share
a small piece of meat with the needy
the greedy lions never care
if they kill innocent people

For them
money is their voice

I HOLD A KEY

Isabell Samuel

What is a key?
What is the use of a key?
I know that some of you think
that is it used
to open or close something

But you are wrong
The key I hold is a key of success
this key helps me to open up my mind
and to close negative attitudes
I can't let it get away
I will keep it day and night
I can't allow anyone to take it from me

I hold this key
for my future
I know that one day
I will get married
and I will keep this key
to open my child's future
I don't want my child to suffer

I hold a key of strength
this key is my special charm
I cannot allow anyone to steal it from me
I know that if it is not held
very carefully
it can close my future
that is why I hold it very tightly

I will always keep it safe
my key is a very special weapon
I will use it to open and close things

I hold a key

For All the Girls Who Come After Me

Janet Chiumia

I need them to be
smart like me
to be humble
and to
always speak the truth.

God expects his children
to speak the truth
and obey him.

I need them to
work hard on their education
so that they can
make their future different.

The Women That I Admire

Janet Chiumia

I admire my mom. She is sweet, innocent, and I can never forget what she has done for me. I am proud of her.

She gave birth to me so that I can see the world. How can I thank you, Mom, for giving me a chance to see the world?

Look what your daughter is doing now! She's growing with intelligence, love, sweetness and working hard in her education.

Thank you, Mom!

Change

Janet Chiumia

You cannot change what you are.
You can only change what you do.

This means a person can only change
what she/he does to improve their behaviour.

Someone cannot change his/her body to be like another's body.

You can also change yourself by listening to other's views.

My Future Will be Different

Juddith Rasheed

My future will be different
because I'm working hard
to be like Mrs. Mwake, my role model

I still say that I have a bright future
no one can take my bright future away

My future will be different
because I'm a strong girl and a hard worker
and I will do
what God has for me to do

My future will be different
because I want to reach what God
has made for me

I will tie my body to the Holy Spirit and
I will laugh at boys
because they want to cut short my bright future

I Hold a Key

Juddith Rasheed

I hold a key
A key
it's our future that can open our minds
the key opens minds
to think critically
I can't throw it away
I always hold it everywhere I'm going
day or night
no one can take away my key

Some people say
our education is a key
that makes us have more power
Our mother, Malawi, says if you teach a girl
you have taught the whole world

That means we are very special
Let's hold our keys tightly
and empower girls, with power

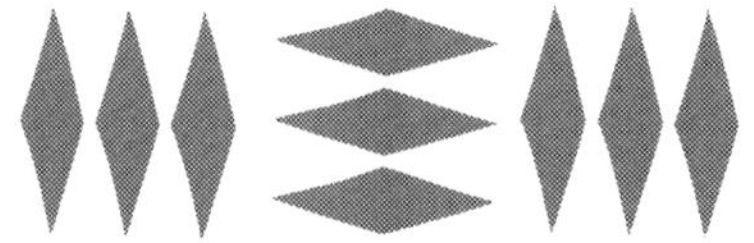

What Am I On Fire For?

Juddith Rasheed

I'm on fire for my education. So many people are suffering because of lack of money. Their parents have no money to pay for school fees for them. But I have a chance to go to school.

I'm on fire for my education. I am working hard to one day have an advanced degree like Dr. Limbikani. We all love this woman, Limbikani, for coming here to teach us many things.

I'm on fire for my education. It's not easy to finish school. We face so many challenges as we are growing up. But we just leave this in the hands of God. God can do anything!

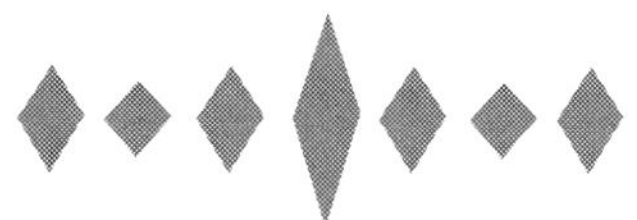

Makeup

Juddith Rasheed

Makeup makes people look smooth and soft. Girls and women believe in makeup to make their faces nice. Some look pretty. Others do not. These are spices for the face. Let's not use makeup, young girls. Use it when you have finished your education.

When girls put on makeup, they can't sleep, they can't drink, they can't eat. And when we ask why, it's to avoid the makeup coming off! Girls, girls, girls. Makeup for what? Let's look the way God created us. Spice, spice, spice. Red, blue, orange, green, grey, pink and apple green, for what? Avoid this, girls.

I Hold a Key

Juliet Phiri

I hold a key
a key of success
a key to my bright future
Oh, my key
without you
I wonder which way I would go

My education can open the door to my future
It can help me get a good job
have a house of my own
and be used to open other doors
Why lose you, key?
You are my best friend forever

But even above this key
I have a real key which can open any door in my life
oh, yes, I'm talking about God
God who can make everything possible
God is the most important key
opening the door to my bright future
that's why love this key
I hold it tightly

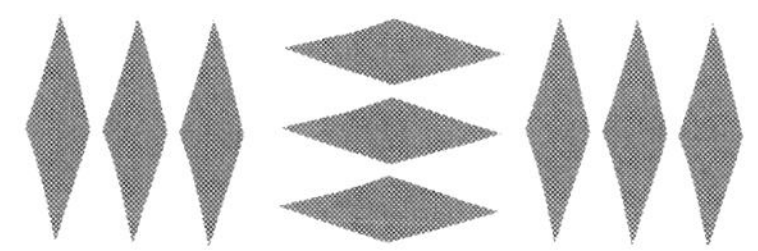

My Future Will Be Different

Juliet Phiri

Oh, yes! My future will be different indeed because I have planned in a good way. I know you might have some questions to ask of me, but I will answer you in this way about the plans I have made. I planned to join Writer's Club and it's been very good because we have learned many things which help us. It's been a good help to all of us as we are growing up.

When I was in nursery school, I was always wishing and hoping that I could go on to primary school. When I was in primary school, I was always wishing and hoping that I could go on to secondary school. Now I am in secondary school and I have two things at the same time helping me to have a good future that is different from others: my school classes and Writer's Club.

For All the Girls Who Come After Me

Juliet Phiri

This is my advice to you girls who come after me… I know you might not listen to me because I am not very old, but I will say it anyway because I am a voice for change. My advice to you is, "Be focused on one thing all the time because it will help you reach your dreams."

Secondly, have confidence as a girl. You have to have high confidence when people don't believe in you. You have to stand. And I know that what I'm fighting for, you will also fight for. I know you will pass through tough situations, but just live with faith that you will get through it, a strong girl. When you are strong, you will smile at your fate because you know good things are coming in the future.

I Hold a Key

Loyce Mpemba

Lock the door
Unlock the door
I hold a key so special
not just for opening a door or a car
but to open my future
a key that will strengthen my faith

We say education is the key to success
not just your key will lead you to success
but hard work will lead you to success

If the key is lost
the door will remain locked
when the key is found
the door will be unlaced

I hold a key
that locks the door
unlocks the door
in and out

I hold a key

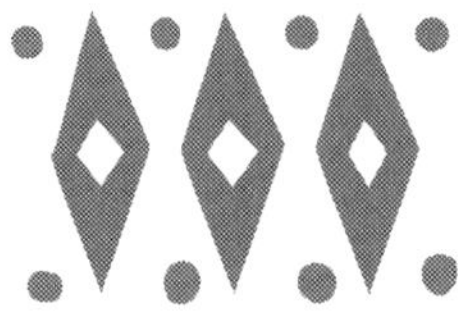

For All the Girls Who Come After Me

Loyce Mpemba

Girls
We are all game changers
I am changing the world through different ways
writing, using my voice, my strength and my uniqueness
we girls have the voices to change the world

For the girls who come after me
do not allow boys to disturb you
because a boy is like a bee
when a bee sees a beautiful flower
it goes there and sucks the juice in it
after that it flies away
to look for another flower

I am repeating this again to you
do not allow boys to disturb you
your future is in your own hands

Use your unique voice to say no
use your unique voice to gain confidence

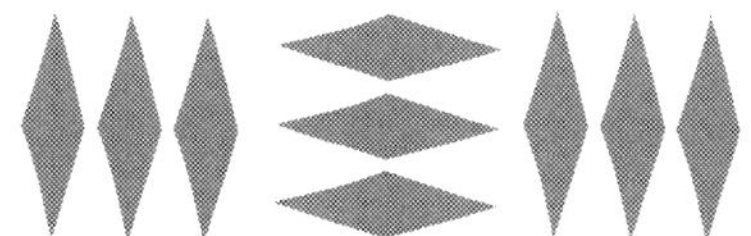

What I'm One Fire For

Madalo Mchazime

I'm on fire for my education and my future.

I'm on fire for it because
I want to have a good job and
become rich so that I can
donate money to the orphanage.

I also hope to buy a
beautiful house
and a blue car.

Change

Madalo Mchazime

"Education is the most powerful weapon which you can use to change the world."

This says that education is the most powerful weapon you can use to change the world. It is true that education is a powerful weapon. It can help you achieve your goals in life because can have a good job in the future, and it helps you have either high or low self-esteem.

In my future job, I want people to respect me. I want to have a private office. I want to be an operation's manager like my mother and father, because both my mother and father are operation's managers.

It Was You

Mercy Chipeta

It was you
who carried me
nine months to your Golgotha
you endured all the pain
you endured all the problems
indeed, it was you

It was you
who brought me
into this world
who cared for me
since I was your bag of pain
waiting for the best day
I remember as my birthday
I can't ever afford to pay back your love

It was you
Today, I am a grown-up girl
and today I am able to have the strength
to speak up and speak out
the voice of change
because I am a game changer

Indeed, it was you
My president? My teacher?
My sister? My friend? My granny?
Oh, no
it was not any of you
but it was my tree of love and care
which bears beautiful fruit that tastes so nice and sweet
I am speaking of my mum

It was you

As A Girl

Mercy Chipeta

As a girl
being empowered is what I'm on fire for
to be given a chance like any boy
given quality education
this is what I want

I want to have that chance to speak out
to live my life for others
for my rights not to be violated
to be employed in any department
and not be looked down on
as a girl

I Feel Strong When

Michelle Mchazime

I feel strong when I sing or drink milk
I feel strong when I go to sleep
or run outside with my friends
I feel strong when I'm joking with friends and relatives
I feel strong when I'm reading books

When Girls are Together

Michelle Mchazime

When girls are together they talk about things they've seen or heard. For example, they talk about things that happened in the past. When girls are together, they talk about school and about nightmares. I see girls laughing and smiling, making each other laugh and being good friends. But what friends do you have, good or bad? Don't have bad friends. They will just teach you bad things!

Party

Monice Mapira

Party, party, party! Everywhere I go, people are talking about you! How special you are that everywhere I go, I hear people talking about you. Are you as special as silver or gold? I have been asking myself, "What do you look like? Are you dark or light in skin? Are you thin or fat?" People are buying drinks and food, expecting a party. What kind of person are you that everyone is talking about you?

Oh! Wait a minute! You aren't a person. But who or what are you really that so many people are buying new clothes, shoes and makeup for you, feeling excited about you? You must be really very special!

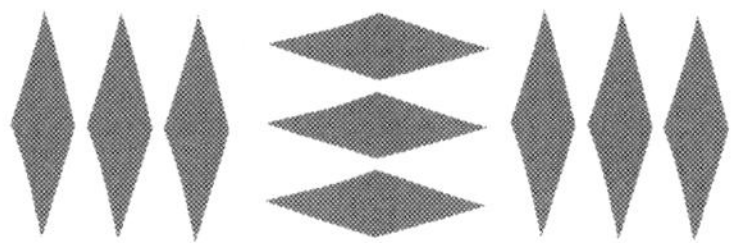

I Hold a Key

Monice Mapira

I hold a key in my hand
to open the treasure of my dream
a dream of success
a dream of education
a key that opens the door of my dream
filled with happiness and joy

The key of my life
I can't afford to lose it
it is so special to me
My eyes are like keys
that unlock the door
to my dreams

I hold a key
that can close my dreams if it is misused
but I can see it opening the door of my dreams
It is like my best friend
more than a best friend
my guardian angel
that guards me on the way
to the door
to my dreams

As We Go

Monice Mapira

As I leave here, I will miss you
and continue loving you all
As I leave here, I will continue writing
using my voice to stop corruption
and to encourage girls to work together in cooperation

As I leave here, I will encourage girls
to work hard at school
and everywhere they go
because I know that we can change the world
through writing
and working hard and
cooperating because together

We can change the world
using our voices
through our writing
together we can

and I will miss you all
thank you for helping me
find my unique voice

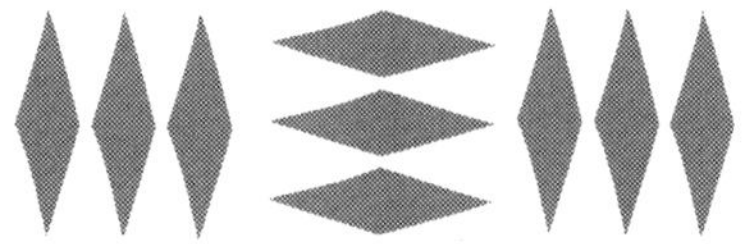

My Keys

Mphatso Major

My eyes are like keys focusing on
my way forward to my goal
That is why they have been there for years
from the day I started to take in the first air

My legs are like keys that help me
to move in a hurry toward my path of opportunities
My legs will only step on the proper path
which was meant for me
In the interest of time, I take care of my legs
so that my legs don't get tired of carrying me

My hands are like keys which were meant to
pull up my socks and dust off my clothes
The minute I fall down
I trust my hands to be there
In times of need
I'm really proud of you, my hand keys

My heart is like a key which was made to
agree to only positive actions and ideas that contribute to
achievements on my way
I trust this key
It has been placed deep inside the other organs

No one can see where it is
for security purposes

As I Leave Here

Mphatso Major

As I leave here
memories of sweet poems and stories
will still rattle in my head
I will miss these strong courageous young girls

As I leave here
I will remember the way my mouth
forced my unique voice out
so that it could be heard by others and bring change

As I leave here
I will remember inspirational words coming out
from fabulous ladies who are doing great things themselves
tools of motivation for others

I know I could not have experienced
this great retreat
if I had not
pushed my voice out

My Mother

Mphatso Major

She is wonderfully made
courageous enough to make new opportunities
She is a hard worker, full of knowledge
She works day and night
coming up with innovative ideas
creating and enabling an environment for her to live in
She deserves to be a leader

She values most her life
She knows who she is
that's why she takes time
to make sure she is progressing
She is making tangible developments
because of what she is composed of
She deserves to be a leader

She loves her culture
She is special to her family and community
She only does what suits her
She does not waste time on expensive things
to make herself more beautiful
She appreciates her beauty
indeed, she deserves to be a leader

My Future Will Be Different

Mwandida Mateyu

Last year I was thinking I'd like to go to school at Bakhita Private Primary School. When I spoke to my mother about it, she said, "No. Stay at the same school you are learning at now because it's the only school that has well qualified teachers who can help you achieve your goals.

I enjoy learning at Mtsiliza Primary School and I'm glad I believed what my mother said about staying there. Staying there allowed me to join Writer's Club where I'm able to write many good stories. It has helped me to build high self-esteem, doing many different things.

Our Visitor

Patumah Binali

Yet another beautiful morning and wonderful day! The fullness of the sun made the day bright. The clouds had scattered across the sky. We all had every reason to thank God. Dressed up in our beautiful, colourful VoiceFlame uniforms, we felt extra beautiful. Aunt Chiko said, "Our visitor will arrive soon, so everyone should take off sweaters so our VoiceFlame shirts show." We all looked at her, surprised. "A visitor?" someone at the back questioned. Aunt Chiko told us she had kept it a secret to surprise us.

A few minutes later, the door opened and there she was. Such a beautiful and shining lady, our pride, the wife of the Vice President of our lovely country, Malawi, Mrs. Mary Chilima! As soon as she arrived, she immediately took the stage. First, she introduced herself. Then she gave us her amazing speech. "No matter what the circumstances may be, you can accomplish anything as long as you're given the chance to."

These are the powerful worlds I'm going to remember as long as I live. She talked of her goals and achievements. She also emphasized good decision making and creative thinking. At the end of her talk, she entertained a few questions. She couldn't stay long because she had a flight to catch. She promised to visit us again! Lastly, we took a group photo with her, our Vice President's wife, Mrs. Chalima.

As I Leave

Patuma Binali

I leave here with lessons
lessons that have changed me
from greater to greatest

As I leave here
I leave with a commitment
to my goals
a commitment to my change
that will be good for Mother Malawi

As I leave here
I leave with a voice
a voice that is unique

As I leave here
I will always remember
that I stand on the shoulders
of those who came before me

As I leave here
I'll move a step forward
to make a ladder for girls
who come after me
because I'm a girl
because I'm strong
because I have a voice
I'll do my best
to change the worst

and leave the rest in God's hands

Change

Regina Jika

"Be the change that you wish to see in the world."
I can be the change
I wish to see changed in the world
the things I wish to change

Every one of us is supposed to change something
If you're not educated, you cannot change anything
If you want to change things
you must think first
and then you can make good decisions

In Malawi,
there are so many things
that need to change like
education
corruption
child abuse
early marriage

Education can
change these things

As a Girl

Regina Jika

As a girl of Malawi
I will do the things that I want
I will be the first person that can change my country

As a girl of writer's club
the girl must write
the girl must learn
the girl must be a teacher
and our voices must be unique

As a girl of education
I will educate all girls
that we must protect ourselves
we must dance
we must sing
and we must do the things
that change ourselves

As a girl

My City

Regina Jika

I have a beautiful city
In my city there are good streets
Along these streets there are good buildings
There are shops, banks, super markets
I love my city

I Hold a Key

Regina Jika

I hold a key
My key is used to open the door
and when you don't have a key
it means you don't want to achieve your goals

I hold a key
I hold a key because education is the key to success
If you're not educated
you won't have the key to anything you want

I hold a key
This key is like me preparing the things
I want to do in the future

I hold a key
If you don't have a key
you don't have vision for the future
If you have a key
you have vision for your future

I hold a key

What I am on Fire For

Regina Jika

I am on fire for education. After I finish school, I want to be a donor and help sick people. It would be so nice to be a doctor and work in Malawi because there are few doctors here. I have a bright future because I have self-confidence, high self-esteem, ambition, and I work hard on many different things.

In Malawi, there are so many jobs that people do. I choose to be a doctor in order to change the world by helping the sick, and by developing my country. When you want things, pray to God to give you everything you need and want. Be a person who helps others. I have a vision to finish school and go to university. I want to work hard on many different things.

My Future Will Be Different

Regina Jika

My future will be different because I will be prayerful
Praying is one thing that every person can do
every day, everywhere

My future will be different because I will be a leader
Every country needs leaders
one of these leaders will be me

My future will be different because
I will be a role model for Malawi

My future will be different because
I will be person who care for street children
I will be a helper

My future will be different because
I will change Malawi

Love Your Neighbour

Sophlet Kawiriza

A long time ago there was a woman named Pepani. She lived with her husband, Madalitso. These two lived in Kanama village. One day, a woman named Nagama and her husband passed by Pepani's house on the way to the vegetable garden. As they were coming home, they stopped in front of Pepani's house because the wife was hungry and thirsty. It was a time when many people didn't have food. They knocked on the door. Knock, knock, knock. Pepani and her husband came to the door. After greeting each other, Pepani asked how they could help the two strangers.

Nagama: Can you share some food and water with us? We've come from far and have nothing.

Pepani: Oh, sorry. I don't have food and water.

Nagama: Oh, please, madam. I can see water inside your home!

Pepani: Get out of my house! I meant I can't share any of my food or water!

Nagama and her husband left the place and began walking home again. Sometime later, Pepani's husband made a serious mistake at work. His boss said he would have to leave his job and just go. Pepani's family starting having many problems after her husband lost his job. One day, the family actually had no more food and Pepani and her husband started begging from house to house.

At one house, Nagama answered.

Nagama: Hello. How are you? How can I help you?

Pepani: I am fine but we have no food. Please, my friend, share with us some food.

Nagama: I know you. Last year I begged you to share some food and water with us. It was you, wasn't it? Yes, it was you. You didn't share anything with us. I mean, you actually refused to share with us!

Pepani: Please, forgive us!

Nagama: Well, I DO forgive you. There should be no problem because I believe, "Love your neighbour as you love yourself."

Pepani and her husband began to cry. It is good to love your neighbour.

Why Me, Lord?

Thandie Chihana

I was just a little girl when my parents died in a car accident. I was left alone and I did not have anyone to support me. I did not have a parent to give me a piece of advice. At that time, I didn't even have a place to live. I was homeless, living on the street.

Six months later, a certain woman talked with me about how my life was going and the discussion went like this:

Me: Hi Auntie, how are you this afternoon?

Auntie: I'm fine, thank you. And you? What are you doing here?

Me: Auntie, it's a long story. I have been staying here for six months since my parents died.

Auntie: OK, dear, I want to take you back to my house and get you back into school. Can I do that?

Me: Oh, that would be such a nice thing! I've really been wanting to go back to school. My dream was always that I could become a doctor.

Auntie: Well, that would be a very nice job for a girl like you! Every girl should go to school, not stay in the streets like this.

Me: Auntie, you speak the truth! But, sadly, some girls are left at home, or living in the streets.

Auntie: OK, my child, it's time to move ahead. Let's go back home to my house and find a solution for your situation.

Me: OK, Auntie. God will surely bless you for what you're doing for me.

Auntie: Don't mention it. It's nothing. And, dear, don't worry too much.

Me: Auntie, you know that God's timing is the best and that is the last words my mother spoke to me before she died.

Auntie: Yes, that is the truth. Let's go home now, to our home.

The Camp

Triphonia Mandowa

My friend! My friend! My friend, Camp!
Are you running away from me?
What have I done to you that you leave me like this?
Were you not happy with me?
But why?
You should know that I'm crying for you
my friend, why are you leaving me?

What will I do if you leave me?
I will suffer and my heart will be broken
You want me to be alone?
Answer me, my friend
What will I do now?
Oh, it's your choice
and all I can say is
Nice journey!

My friend, Camp
I think we will meet again
but when?
From you, friend, I have learned more things
than I have ever learned before
Goodbye!
Goodbye!
Goodbye, my friend, Camp.

My Lost Key

Triphonia Mandowa

My lost key
Where are you?
I look for you everywhere,
my house remains locked
How can I get in without you?
Please, please come back home, my key

My lost key
You symbolise different things to me
Now where can I go without you?
You are the direction of my future
Oh, no! What kind of future will mine be
without you?

My lost key
I'm crying for you
Please come back because
you are the one who shall bring happiness
to my family

My Lovely Enemy

Triphonia Mandowa

My lovely enemy
Where are you?
I've been looking for you
for a long time
I miss you so much
can you come here, please?
I want to see you
my lovely enemy

My lovely enemy
Now I see that you are
a good friend
I want you to forgive me
for what I have done to you
Please, please forget all the past
my lovely enemy

You made to be an honourable person
and you made many people rich
What kind of love do you have
my lovely enemy

Now I've found you
you are just sitting there waiting for me
Oh, you are my education
so please, stay close with me
my lovely enemy

For All the Girls Who Come After Me

Twambilire Kamwaza

Girls, girls
Don't allow them to
boss you around like that

I do this for all the girls
who come after me
so that they can see
an example of what it feels like
to reach your goals

The ball is in your hands
You should remember to remember
what I remember to remember
for I stand for those who fall
and are failing to
stand up for themselves

And for all the girls
who come after me
I tell them to rise up
and say no to abuse

When Women Are Together

Twambilire Kamwaza

It was a hot Sunday when some women, about seven or eight of them, sat under a cinderella tree. At first, I thought it was a meeting. I thought about it over and over again while I sat on my verandah feeling the fresh air and gazing at the trees. The women were near the verandah. Some were bathed and some were not, but they seemed not to mind either way. I wanted to listen to their conversation so badly! I decided the best way I could do this was to eavesdrop, so I squeezed myself up to the edge of the verandah.

To my surprise, I saw our neighbour, who was busy complaining about her husband, Mr. William. She said, "I can't believe my husband! He's always coming home late and when I ask him, he says there was too much work to do." I was not surprised to hear this because my mom also often comes home late. But another woman said, "I always see your husband drinking alcohol with his friends after work."

When women are together, they talk.

What Am I On Fire For?

Veritah Amos

It was a Monday ending when my mum and dad were not home and I was watching television. I heard someone open the door and when I ran to see who it was, I saw it was my parents. About an hour later, my dad called me and asked me what I was doing. I told him I was just watching television. He said, "You're a stupid child. What will your future be and what are you on fire for?"

I didn't answer him so he told me to go to my room and study. I was thinking, like, "I don't want to do so!" Then my mum said, "Look at me and your dad. We're educated people and we want you to be the same."

I left but about a month later I realised that my parents were speaking the truth. I needed to change my behavior regarding television. So I wrote a letter to my parents and told them I was not a stupid child any longer. I told them I am on fire for my goal of becoming an accountant and a lawyer.

Environment

Veritah Amos

One day I found myself in the forest because I had wandered from my path. It was quiet like a graveyard there and the trees were many. The green leaves were thick and the fallen ones on the ground were thick like a carpet. Since the time of Adam and Eve, no one had passed this way. I saw wild roses meandering as they grew. I picked one from the bush and I began to run, unaware that I was getting lost further from home in this wild environment.

"What is this environment and how can it help me?" I wondered. As I thought about it, I realised this environment gives me oxygen for breathing. It gives me fossil fuel for cooking. "Oh!" I wondered, "How was this amazing environment created? Was it by God? Was it created by man? Oh, how can I get the answers?" I wondered. I began to realise it was naturally created by God and is surrounded by humans so that they can take care of it.

I will never forget about this forest. It has become like a best friend to me. I eventually decided to live there and to not return back home. I will always take care of the forest because it is my home now.

Do you have a home like mine? Do you have a best friend like mine? Do not wait. Go and find yours. The path and life that is right for you will be the best.

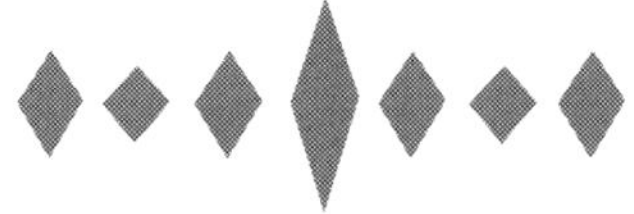

My Future Will Be Different

Veritah Amos

Once upon a time there was no technology like phones, televisions, etc. People of that time were able to communicate with each other by the means of letters sent to each other. When people went further with their education and development, things changed, little by little. I believe that my future will be different because the technology that will continue to be discovered and developed will make the world change.

If technology changes the world, what about me? I really, really hope that my future will not be the same. Just like for Anastasia Msosa, Chief Justice of Malawi, who faced many problems in her school time, but now things have changed for her and she has a better life. I have learned and been taught how life goes and how as a girl you can be discriminated against and left out by society. But that doesn't mean your future can't be different from the past. With hard work, my future will be different.

A Blessing

Mary Tuchscherer

May all voices
be set free
to awaken strength
to receive education
to pursue dreams
to ignite flames
to remove silence
to speak truth
to find purpose
to take action
to change lives

A note from the editor

Lizabeth Rogers

When my friend Deborah Gray sent me a message suggesting that I might be a good choice for editor of this book, I knew instantly that she was right. Not because I'm the best editor - but because I trust Deborah. Somewhere, deep in my gut, I knew I had to contact Mary and offer my help.

I've anguished and languished over the essays and poetry born from the extraordinary minds of these women - the seeds of thought, creativity and inspiration, fed and nurtured by Mary Tuchscherer and VoiceFlame. I started, stopped, started again, crumbled then picked myself up and started once more. This book is a product of their work, not mine. I've merely packaged the beauty that they have created.

I live an idyllic life, lucky in myriad ways to have tools and opportunities at my disposal to imagine, create and spew art.

These though, are women who struggle every day to get the education I so blithely took for granted. The telling of their stories and the wings that raise their poetry into flight are extraordinary.

Allow yourself to read, and re-read them, as I have.

You, too, will be blessed.